The Complete
LIVE AND *LEARN*
and
Pass It On

The Complete
LIVE AND *LEARN*
and
Pass It On

H. Jackson Brown, Jr.

Published by
THOMAS NELSON
Since 1798
www.thomasnelson.com

Published in Nashville, Tennessee, by Thomas Nelson, Inc.

Art Direction and Design by Mary Hooper.

Library of Congress Cataloging-in-Publication Data

The complete live and learn and pass it on / written and compiled by
H. Jackson Brown, Jr.
    p. cm.
    ISBN 1-4016-0331-9
    1. Life cycle, Human—Miscellanea. 2. Developmental psychology—Miscellanea.
3. Maturation (Psychology)—Miscellanea. I. Brown, H. Jackson, 1940- .
HQ799.95.L55 1991   91-32132
158'.1—dc20   CIP

Printed in Canada

07 08 09 10 TPC 5 4 3 2 1

INTRODUCTION

On the morning of my fifty-first birthday I gave myself the assignment of jotting down a few of the important things that more than half a century of living had taught me.

I found this exercise so instructive and enjoyable that I made it a regular Sunday morning project. Later, I read the list to a friend over lunch and he said it was an idea he'd like to try. Other friends and acquaintances soon joined in. That led to interviews with kindergarten kids, high school students, young married couples, and senior citizens. Editing these entries convinced me that wisdom knows no age and that truth is truth no matter where you find it.

The contributors to *The Complete Live and Learn and*

Pass It On represent all ages and every economic and social background. They would not consider themselves philosophers or gurus, yet here, in just a sentence or two, they offer us worlds of wisdom.

As you read these observations, you will get a glimpse now and then of lonely hearts and lost hopes. But what ultimately comes through is a sense of cheerfulness, resolve, and the importance of keeping things in perspective. A forty-two-year-old father writes, "I've learned that a shoeshine box made by my eight-year-old son at Vacation Bible School is my most prized possession." That's as powerful a statement about priorities and what makes life worth living as you will ever read.

The seventeeth-century English clergyman Thomas Fuller wrote, "If you have knowledge, let others light their candle at it." Thanks to these people who have shared their "life's lessons" with me, my candle now burns with a lively flame. I invite you to light your candle from mine. By holding them together, we'll illuminate our own path as well as signal a direction for those who follow.

H. J. B.
Tall Pine Lodge
Fernvale, Tennessee

Other Books by H. Jackson Brown, Jr.

Life's Little Instruction Book®
(volumes I, II, and III)

Live and Learn and Pass It On
(volumes I, II, and III)

Complete Life's Little Instruction Book

Highlighted in Yellow
(with Rochelle Pennington)

For Rosemary and Adam,
with love.

Volume I

I've learned that life is like a scooter car; not much happens unless you do some pedaling. — AGE 79

• • •

I've learned that when you remodel, everything costs twice as much and takes twice as long as you think it will. — AGE 48

• • •

I've learned that my daddy can say a lot of words I can't. — AGE 8

• • •

I've learned that it doesn't cost anything to be nice. — AGE 66

I've learned that if someone says something unkind about me, I must live so that no one will believe it. —AGE 39

• • •

I've learned that most of the things I worry about never happen. —AGE 64

• • •

I've learned that a patrol car behind me always makes me nervous. —AGE 25

• • •

I've learned that homemade Toll House cookies should be eaten while still warm. —AGE 29

I've learned that you can get by on charm for about fifteen minutes. After that, you'd better know something. —AGE 46

• • •

I've learned that no one has a clue about what the stock market is going to do. —AGE 51

• • •

I've learned that if you spread the peas out on your plate, it looks like you ate more. —AGE 6

• • •

I've learned that couples without children always know just how you should raise yours. —AGE 29

I've learned that every great achievement was once considered impossible. —AGE 47

• • •

I've learned that the great challenge of life is to decide what's important and to disregard everything else. —AGE 51

• • •

I've learned that getting fired can be the best thing that can happen to you. —AGE 42

• • •

I've learned that just when I get my room the way I like it, Mom makes me clean it up.
—AGE 13

I've learned that almost no quality product sells for a cheap price. –AGE 52

• • •

I've learned that you shouldn't compare yourself to the best others can do, but to the best you can do. –AGE 68

• • •

I've learned that the more creative you are, the more things you notice. –AGE 51

• • •

I've learned that my gas tank is always on empty when I'm late for an important meeting. –AGE 32

I've learned that life challenges us with the fact that everything can be done better. –AGE 57

• • •

I've learned that it doesn't do any good to buy expensive tools if I can never find them. –AGE 41

• • •

I've learned that if you like garlic salt and Tabasco sauce you can make almost anything taste good. –AGE 52

• • •

I've learned that after age 50 you get the furniture disease. That's when your chest falls into your drawers. –AGE 53

I've learned that it's hard to argue with someone when they're right. –AGE 38

• • •

I've learned that you shouldn't call a $100 meeting to solve a $10 problem. –AGE 55

• • •

I've learned that car salesmen size up prospects by looking at the quality of their shoes and watches. –AGE 52

• • •

I've learned that you never outgrow the enjoyment of browsing in toy departments. –AGE 61

I've learned that at least once in his life, a man makes a fool of himself over a woman. —AGE 46

• • •

I've learned that trust is the single most important factor in both personal and professional relationships. —AGE 20

• • •

I've learned that marrying for money is the hardest way to get it. —AGE 42

• • •

I've learned that if you take good care of your employees, they will take good care of your customers. —AGE 49

I've learned that you can't hide a piece of broccoli in a glass of milk. –AGE 7

I've learned that nothing of value comes without effort. −AGE 64

• • •

I've learned that even the simplest task can be meaningful if I do it in the right spirit. −AGE 72

• • •

I've learned that the best thing about growing older is that now I don't feel the need to impress anyone. −AGE 79

• • •

I've learned that the size of your biceps has very little to do with your popularity and success after high school. −AGE 50

I've learned that when my brother leaves for college, I get everything. —AGE 14

• • •

I've learned that enthusiasm is caught, not taught. —AGE 51

• • •

I've learned that if you want to get even with someone at camp, rub their underwear in poison ivy. —AGE 11

• • •

I've learned that even a doctor with the best training and intentions can be wrong about a diagnosis. —AGE 58

I've learned that a person is only as good as his or her word. –AGE 90

• • •

I've learned that you can be in love with four girls at the same time. –AGE 9

• • •

I've learned that lying in the cool green grass and looking at the sky makes you feel so good.
–AGE 14

• • •

I've learned that it's better to be married to someone with a good nature than a good physique. –AGE 39

14

I've learned that when you can be either brilliant or pleasant, choose pleasant. —AGE 53

• • •

I've learned that untold treasures are found in the imagination of a child. —AGE 30

• • •

I've learned that if you laugh and drink soda pop at the same time, it will come out your nose. —AGE 7

• • •

I've learned that you should always leave loved ones with loving words. It could be the last time you see them. —AGE 60

I've learned that children and grandparents are natural allies. —AGE 46

. . .

I've learned that the ache of unfulfilled dreams is the worst pain of all. —AGE 51

. . .

I've learned that you can do something in an instant that will give you a heartache for life. —AGE 27

. . .

I've learned that a teenager's biggest fear is the fear of a broken heart. —AGE 16

I've learned that if I'm in trouble at school, I'm in more trouble at home. —AGE 11

. . .

I've learned that no matter how thin you slice it, there are always two sides. —AGE 58

. . .

I've learned that regardless of color or age, we all need about the same amount of love. —AGE 37

. . .

I've learned that a person's degree of self-confidence greatly determines his success. —AGE 42

I've learned that generous people seldom have emotional and mental problems. –AGE 51

• • •

I've learned that in every face-to-face encounter, regardless of how brief, we leave something behind. –AGE 45

• • •

I've learned that if you hire mediocre people, they will hire mediocre people. –AGE 53

• • •

I've learned that it's not what happens to people that's important. It's what they do about it. –AGE 10

I've learned that even when I have pains,
I don't have to be a pain. –AGE 82

• • •

I've learned that I shouldn't go grocery
shopping when I'm hungry. –AGE 38

• • •

I've learned that even when you schedule a
doctor's appointment at 8:00 a.m., you still
have to wait an hour. –AGE 42

• • •

I've learned that one of the sweetest smells I
know is my husband's clean-shaven face in the
morning. –AGE 39

I've learned that success is more often the result of hard work than of talent. —AGE 59

• • •

I've learned that I should never praise my mother's cooking when I'm eating something fixed by my wife. —AGE 27

• • •

I've learned that silent company is often more healing than words of advice. —AGE 24

• • •

I've learned that the quickest way to meet people is to pick up the wrong golf ball on the golf course. —AGE 43

I've learned that it makes me sad when I'm the last one chosen for a team. —AGE 9

• • •

I've learned that nothing really bad happens when you tear those little "do not remove" tags from pillows. —AGE 31

• • •

I've learned that your teenage years are comprised of tribulations, confusion, agony, and love. —AGE 15

• • •

I've learned that I cannot expect others to solve my problems. —AGE 34

I've learned that if you pursue happiness, it will elude you. But if you focus on your family, the needs of others, your work, meeting new people, and doing the very best you can, happiness will find you. –AGE 65

• • •

I've learned that motel mattresses are better on the side away from the phone. –AGE 50

• • •

I've learned that if you care, it shows. –AGE 30

• • •

I've learned that you need to let your children be children. –AGE 38

I've learned that eating chocolate won't solve your problems, but it doesn't hurt anything either. –AGE 28

• • •

I've learned that my mother is always happy to see me. –AGE 44

• • •

I've learned that regardless of your relationship with your parents, you miss them terribly after they die. –AGE 53

• • •

I've learned that you should never go to bed with an argument unsettled. –AGE 73

I've learned that you shouldn't go through life with a catcher's mitt on both hands. You need to be able to throw something back. —AGE 66

I've learned that the best way to lose a friend is to lend him money.   −AGE 36

. . .

I've learned that education, experience, and memories are three things no one can take away from you.   −AGE 67

. . .

I've learned that it's taking me a long time to become the person I want to be.   −AGE 51

. . .

I've learned that Mom wouldn't like my boyfriend even if he were captain of the football team and sang in the church choir.   −AGE 17

I've learned that kindness is more important than perfection. —AGE 70

• • •

I've learned that nothing is more fun than a job you enjoy. —AGE 29

• • •

I've learned that when your husband cooks, you should compliment everything he fixes.
—AGE 77

• • •

I've learned that if you look for the worst in life and in people, you'll find it. But if you look for the best, you'll find that instead. —AGE 66

I've learned that more comfort doesn't necessarily mean more happiness. —AGE 55

• • •

I've learned that the greater a person's sense of guilt, the greater his need to cast blame on others. —AGE 46

• • •

I've learned that you shouldn't look back except to learn. —AGE 70

• • •

I've learned that when traveling overseas, it's best to carry a good supply of American-made toilet paper. —AGE 54

I've learned that it's best not to quit at quitting time. −AGE 37

• • •

I've learned that my children's birthdays make me feel older than my own birthday does.
−AGE 46

• • •

I've learned that men who wear bow ties are usually great dancers. −AGE 34

• • •

I've learned that when my daddy kisses me in the mornings, he smells like a piece of Jolly Rancher candy. −AGE 10

I've learned that you can't tell how far a frog can jump just by looking at him.   –AGE 79

• • •

I've learned that when someone tells you it's the principle of the thing and not the money, it's usually the money.   –AGE 65

• • •

I've learned that if I eat donuts today I wear them tomorrow.   –AGE 34

• • •

I've learned that it is very painful to see my negative personality traits alive in my children.   –AGE 39

I've learned that whenever I take a fishing trip, the guy who runs the bait shop always says, "Gee, you should have been here yesterday." –AGE 43

• • •

I've learned that the secret of growing old gracefully is never to lose your enthusiasm for meeting new people and seeing new places. –AGE 75

• • •

I've learned that when you read bedtime stories, kids really do notice if you use the same voice for the handsome prince that you used for the evil ogre the night before. –AGE 29

I've learned that I wish my mother hadn't let me stop taking piano lessons. —AGE 41

. . .

I've learned that when my parents are in a bad mood, it's best to agree to everything they say or things get nasty. —AGE 16

. . .

I've learned that life sometimes gives you a second chance. —AGE 62

. . .

I've learned that when I drop a slice of bread with jelly on it, it always lands jelly-side down. —AGE 33

I've learned that having a baby doesn't solve marital problems. –AGE 24

• • •

I've learned that beyond a certain comfortable style of living, the more material things you have, the less freedom you have. –AGE 62

• • •

I've learned that the worst pain is watching someone else in pain. –AGE 46

• • •

I've learned that it pays to believe in miracles. And to tell the truth, I've seen several. –AGE 73

I've learned that anger manages everything poorly.   -AGE 53

• • •

I've learned that most people are honest.   -AGE 82

• • •

I've learned that if you're riding in a pickup truck with two other people, you should either drive or sit in the middle. The person riding shotgun has to get out to open and close all the gates.   -AGE 19

• • •

I've learned that nothing is more soothing than the warm sun on your face.   -AGE 29

I've learned that it's OK to enjoy your success, but you should never quite believe it.

–AGE 63

• • •

I've learned that the older I get, the more pretty girls I remember kissing as a young man. –AGE 84

• • •

I've learned that a person's posture says a lot about his or her self-confidence. –AGE 59

• • •

I've learned that a good reputation is a person's greatest asset. –AGE 74

I've learned that attractiveness is a positive, caring attitude and has nothing to do with face lifts or nose jobs. –AGE 56

. . .

I've learned that if your children feel safe, wanted, and loved, you are a successful parent. –AGE 39

. . .

I've learned that some money costs too much.
–AGE 51

. . .

I've learned that you shouldn't look for romance where you work. –AGE 31

I've learned that you know your husband still
loves you when there are two brownies left
and he takes the smaller one. —AGE 39

I've learned that when you have an argument with your spouse, the first one who says, "I'm sorry I hurt your feelings; please forgive me," is the winner. —AGE 51

• • •

I've learned that everyone is attractive when they smile. —AGE 51

• • •

I've learned that brushing my child's hair is one of life's great pleasures. —AGE 29

• • •

I've learned that it's a lot easier to react than it is to think. —AGE 55

I've learned that although parents and elders may lecture and discipline you, you will later realize that it was because they cared. –AGE 15

• • •

I've learned that you never ask a tire salesman if you need new tires. –AGE 44

• • •

I've learned that wealthy people are no happier than those of modest means. –AGE 68

• • •

I've learned that to experience the wonder of life through the eyes of a child is the most rewarding feeling in the world. –AGE 30

I've learned that the person with big dreams is more powerful than one with all the facts. –AGE 51

. . .

I've learned that a sunroof is worth the extra cost. –AGE 29

. . .

I've learned that any activity becomes creative when you try to do it better than you did it before. –AGE 48

. . .

I've learned that you should never pay for a job until it's completed. –AGE 48

I've learned that you can't hug your kids too much. −AGE 54

• • •

I've learned that people are about as happy as they decide to be. −AGE 79

• • •

I've learned that the best and quickest way to appreciate other people is to try and do their job. −AGE 51

• • •

I've learned that "Today's Featured Items" is a euphemism for "Things We Need To Get Rid Of." −AGE 19

I've learned that it's easier to stay out of trouble than to get out of trouble.   –AGE 14

• • •

I've learned that when you have the choice of eating at a table or at the counter in a coffee shop, choose the counter. The service will be faster, the food hotter, and the conversation livelier.   –AGE 46

• • •

I've learned that there are four ages of a man: (1) when he believes in Santa Claus, (2) when he doesn't believe in Santa Claus, (3) when he is Santa Claus, and (4) when he looks like Santa Claus. –AGE 51

I've learned that singing "Amazing Grace" can lift my spirits for hours. —AGE 49

• • •

I've learned that you must fight for the things you believe in. —AGE 70

• • •

I've learned that in the stock market, bulls make money and bears make money, but hogs get slaughtered. —AGE 45

• • •

I've learned that you shouldn't marry someone who has more problems than you. —AGE 31

I've learned that days are long, but life is short. –AGE 88

• • •

I've learned that being a success at the office is not worth it if it means being a failure at home. –AGE 51

• • •

I've learned that you can teach yourself anything by reading. –AGE 78

• • •

I've learned that children are the best teachers of creativity, persistence, and unconditional love. –AGE 37

I've learned that you learn most from people who are learning themselves. —AGE 62

• • •

I've learned that when Mommy and Daddy shout at each other, it scares me. —AGE 5

• • •

I've learned that when bad times come, you can let them make you bitter or use them to make you better. —AGE 75

• • •

I've learned that women with double first names usually know how to make a terrific peach cobbler. —AGE 29

I've learned that humming a tune when you're upset can ease your mind. −AGE 14

• • •

I've learned that parents are very hard to live with. −AGE 12

• • •

I've learned that when making a decision, "no" is more easily changed to "yes" than "yes" is changed to "no". −AGE 55

• • •

I've learned that I don't feel my age as long as I focus on my dreams instead of my regrets.

−AGE 83

I've learned that the simple things are often the most satisfying. —AGE 63

• • •

I've learned that you should never sign a contract with blank spaces. —AGE 47

• • •

I've learned that if you allow people to make you angry, you have let them conquer you. —AGE 54

• • •

I've learned that when I eat fish sticks, they help me swim faster because they're fish. —AGE 7

The Complete Live and Learn and Pass It On

I've learned that encouragement from a good teacher can turn a student's life around. —AGE 44

• • •

I've learned that I have never regretted being too generous, but often regretted not being generous enough. —AGE 76

• • •

I've learned that when I wave to people in the country, they almost always stop what they're doing and wave back. —AGE 9

• • •

I've learned that nothing tastes as good as vegetables from your own garden. —AGE 62

I've learned that to love and be loved is the greatest joy in the world. –AGE 78

• • •

I've learned that children want their parents' attention and will go to extreme lengths to get it. –AGE 37

• • •

I've learned that how you do your work is a portrait of yourself. –AGE 64

• • •

I've learned that successful living is like playing a violin—it must be practiced daily.
–AGE 70

I've learned that whenever I decide something with kindness, I usually make the right decision. —AGE 66

I've learned that you can make someone's day by simply sending them a little card. –AGE 44

• • •

I've learned that if your life is free of failures, you're probably not taking enough risks. –AGE 42

• • •

I've learned that every time I'm on a trip I wish I were home, and every time I'm at home I wish I were on a trip. –AGE 59

• • •

I've learned that the person who says something can't be done is often interrupted by someone doing it. –AGE 43

I've learned that when I grow up, I'm going to be an artist. It's in my blood. —AGE 8

• • •

I've learned that you never ask a lady her age, her weight, or what's in her purse. —AGE 68

• • •

I've learned that it's just as important to forget a wrong as it is to remember a kindness.
—AGE 72

• • •

I've learned that if you wait until retirement to really start living, you've waited too long.
—AGE 67

I've learned that if I don't try new things,
I won't learn new things. —AGE 38

• • •

I've learned that total pleasure is a good book,
a soft couch, and a cat curled up beside you.
—AGE 50

• • •

I've learned that my success stops when I do.
—AGE 58

• • •

I've learned that if you keep doing what you've
always done, you'll keep getting what you've
always gotten. —AGE 51

I've learned that the best way to cheer up
yourself is to cheer up someone else. −AGE 13

• • •

I've learned that a full life is not determined
by how long you live, but how well. −AGE 66

• • •

I've learned that to become successful, it
helps to dress the part. −AGE 28

• • •

I've learned that violence on television
and in the movies is so graphic and extreme
that it's numbing our children to pain and
suffering in the real world. −AGE 59

I've learned that you should never jump out of a second story window using a sheet for a parachute. —AGE 10

• • •

I've learned that you should treat everyone with respect, and demand respect in return.
—AGE 51

• • •

I've learned that milk tastes best when you drink it straight out of the plastic jug. —AGE 48

• • •

I've learned that even small children have a right to privacy. —AGE 33

I've learned that optimists live longer than pessimists. That's why I'm an optimist. –AGE 84

• • •

I've learned that although it's hard to admit it, I'm secretly glad my parents are strict with me. –AGE 15

• • •

I've learned that my best friends are usually the ones who get me in trouble. –AGE 11

• • •

I've learned that if you stay focused on yourself, you are guaranteed to be miserable. –AGE 71

I've learned that you can keep going long after you think you can't. –AGE 69

• • •

I've learned that good health is true wealth. –AGE 77

• • •

I've learned that if you want decent airline food, call ahead and ask for a low-sodium meal. It's always better than the regular fare. –AGE 42

• • •

I've learned that the tooth fairy doesn't always come. Sometimes he's broke. –AGE 8

I've learned that there are two things essential to a happy marriage—separate checking accounts and separate bathrooms. –AGE 36

• • •

I've learned that young people need old people's love, respect, and knowledge of life, and that old people need the love, respect, and strength of young people. –AGE 85

• • •

I've learned that you can ruin a good relationship with a professional person such as a doctor, a lawyer, or a CPA when you assume he or she wants to talk shop after hours. –AGE 40

I've learned that any place I haven't visited offers the same potential for adventure and excitement as any other. –AGE 45

• • •

I've learned that you shouldn't handcuff yourself to your little brother and dare him to swallow the key. –AGE 11

• • •

I've learned that there are no unimportant acts of kindness. –AGE 51

• • •

I've learned that you should keep your promises no matter what. –AGE 81

I've learned that people are never sneaky in only one area of their life. –AGE 40

• • •

I've learned that regardless of which bank teller's line you get in, the other ones move faster. –AGE 32

• • •

I've learned that on the one day I'm late for work, that's the one morning my boss is early.
–AGE 38

• • •

I've learned that as long as I have my health, older is better than younger. –AGE 72

I've learned that to insure rain, schedule an outdoor wedding. –AGE 52

. . .

I've learned that there's no substitute for good manners. –AGE 37

. . .

I've learned that if you talk on the phone too long with a girl, your parents suspect something is going on. –AGE 11

. . .

I've learned that I can't tell the difference between a $20 bottle of wine and a $40 bottle of wine. –AGE 39

I've learned that the two happiest days of my life were the day I bought my boat and the day I sold my boat. —AGE 42

I've learned that if you can't forgive and forget, you can at least forgive and move on.

–AGE 77

• • •

I've learned that, ultimately, takers lose and givers win.   –AGE 58

• • •

I've learned that I love my brother because he sticks up for me.   –AGE 9

• • •

I've learned that if you're the boss and you stop rowing, you shouldn't be surprised if everyone else rests too.   –AGE 59

I've learned that everyone can afford to be generous with praise. It's not something available only to the well-to-do. –AGE 76

• • •

I've learned that what you are thinking about, you are becoming. –AGE 55

• • •

I've learned that it's harmful for parents to live out their athletic fantasies through their children. –AGE 43

• • •

I've learned that I should never try out a new recipe on guests. –AGE 24

I've learned that people treat me the way I allow them to treat me. –AGE 47

• • •

I've learned that my greatest fear is that in later years I'll look back at a long list of things I "never got around to." –AGE 30

• • •

I've learned that what my grandmother said was true: time does seem to go faster the older you get. –AGE 48

• • •

I've learned that if I don't know the answer, it's best to say, "I don't know." –AGE 59

I've learned that if you don't have a will or do some estate planning, the government and lawyers become your heirs. —AGE 62

• • •

I've learned that it takes a lot more creativity to find out what's right than what's wrong. —AGE 38

• • •

I've learned that when you buy an old drafty house, you spend more time at the hardware store than you do at home. —AGE 46

• • •

I've learned that expensive new silk ties are the only ones that attract spaghetti sauce. —AGE 44

I've learned that you shouldn't brag about one of your children in the presence of another. –AGE 77

• • •

I've learned that a daily twenty-minute walk is the easiest and most beneficial thing you can do for your health. –AGE 52

• • •

I've learned that all transactions and relationships are enriched by courtesy. –AGE 59

• • •

I've learned that I don't make many mistakes with my mouth shut. –AGE 33

I've learned that an insatiable curiosity is important to never feeling old. —AGE 71

• • •

I've learned that big problems always start out small. —AGE 20

• • •

I've learned that you can't expect your children to listen to your advice and ignore your example. —AGE 51

• • •

I've learned that moving away from my closest friends was much, much harder to do than I ever thought it would be. —AGE 26

I've learned that girls sweat just as much as boys. −AGE 11

• • •

I've learned that I will always be seeking my parents' approval. −AGE 39

• • •

I've learned that happiness is like perfume: you can't give it away without getting a little on yourself. −AGE 59

• • •

I've learned that the exact size drill bit I need is always the one that's missing from the set.

−AGE 46

I've learned that honesty in little things is not a little thing. —AGE 75

• • •

I've learned that what a child learns at home lasts until the grave. —AGE 85

• • •

I've learned that the time to read the instructions is before you try to put the swing set together. —AGE 32

• • •

I've learned that if a child is not getting love and attention at home, he will go somewhere else to find them. —AGE 46

I've learned that being a grandparent is God's compensation for growing older.   –AGE 64

• • •

I've learned that there's no elevator to success. You have to take the stairs.   –AGE 48

• • •

I've learned that if you don't focus on the money but on doing a good job, the money will come.   –AGE 59

• • •

I've learned that if your mother made pimento cheese with Miracle Whip, you don't like it when it's made with mayonnaise.   –AGE 32

I've learned that the more a child feels valued, the better his values will be. −AGE 39

• • •

I've learned that the only thing you owe life is to become the best you can be. −AGE 31

• • •

I've learned that you can't judge boys by the way they look. −AGE 12

• • •

I've learned that you can tell a lot about a man by the way he handles these three things: a rainy holiday, lost luggage, and tangled Christmas tree lights. −AGE 52

I've learned that if you smile at people, they will almost always smile back. –AGE 81

• • •

I've learned that being too quick to judge someone can deprive you of a great encounter and the possibility of a wonderful long-term relationship. –AGE 40

• • •

I've learned that it takes very little extra effort to be considered outstanding. –AGE 46

• • •

I've learned that we are responsible for what we do, no matter how we feel. –AGE 51

I've learned that although there may be reasons to be cynical, it never helps correct the situation. —AGE 51

. . .

I've learned that I can't visit a bookstore without buying something. —AGE 44

. . .

I've learned that you should get all estimates in writing. —AGE 35

. . .

I've learned that I should make the little decisions with my head and the big decisions with my heart. —AGE 52

I've learned that the IRS makes mistakes. –AGE 38

• • •

I've learned that I have never been bored in the presence of a cheerful person. –AGE 63

• • •

I've learned that there is always someone who cares. –AGE 75

• • •

I've learned that when a man with money meets a man with experience, the man with experience ends up with the money and the man with the money ends up with experience.
–AGE 59

I've learned that you can't pay somebody to practice for you. —AGE 52

I've learned that categorizing people is destructive and unfair. –AGE 39

• • •

I've learned that age is important only if you are a cheese. –AGE 76

• • •

I've learned that everything sounds romantic in a foreign language, no matter what is said.
–AGE 27

• • •

I've learned that if you want to do something positive for your children, try to improve your marriage. –AGE 61

I've learned that going the extra mile puts you miles ahead of your competition. –AGE 66

. . .

I've learned that it's easier to keep up than to catch up. –AGE 46

. . .

I've learned that how people treat me is more a reflection of how they see themselves than how they see me. –AGE 49

. . .

I've learned that parents will never understand the importance of a telephone to a teenager. –AGE 16

I've learned that choices made in adolescence
have long-term consequences.   –AGE 49

• • •

I've learned that if you depend on others
to make you happy, you'll be endlessly
disappointed. –AGE 60

• • •

I've learned that a fulfilled life is not possible
without friends. –AGE 39

• • •

I've learned that the quality of the service in a
hotel is in direct proportion to the thickness of
the towels. –AGE 46

I've learned that when I come home from a date, I'm always glad to see that my parents have left the porch light on for me. –AGE 17

• • •

I've learned that you should invest in your family first and in your career second. –AGE 48

• • •

I've learned that it is impossible to teach without learning something yourself. –AGE 51

• • •

I've learned that when wearing suspenders with one strap down, you need to be careful when going to the bathroom. –AGE 10

I've learned that if there were no problems, there would be no opportunities. –AGE 19

• • •

I've learned that you shouldn't fight a battle if there's nothing to win. –AGE 53

• • •

I've learned that people are more influenced by how much I care than by how much I know. –AGE 54

• • •

I've learned that an economist is the only person who can be right just 10 percent of the time and still get a paycheck. –AGE 62

I've learned that no one makes potato salad as good as Mom's. —AGE 51

• • •

I've learned that the body has a miraculous capacity to heal itself. —AGE 78

• • •

I've learned that the most creative ideas often come from beginners and not the experts.
—AGE 62

• • •

I've learned that deciding who you marry is the most important decision you'll ever make.
—AGE 92

I've learned not to kiss and tell. —AGE 15

• • •

I've learned that nothing gives you freedom like a few bucks in the bank. —AGE 48

• • •

I've learned that everyone has something to teach. —AGE 51

• • •

I've learned that when someone is looking sad or seems as if something bad has happened, don't say "What's the matter?" or "What's wrong?" say "Do you want to talk about it? I'm here for you." —AGE 14

I've learned that if you want to know who's the boss in a family, just check to see who holds the TV remote control. –AGE 48

. . .

I've learned that envy is the enemy of happiness. –AGE 73

. . .

I've learned that everyone can use a prayer.
–AGE 72

. . .

I've learned that love is a great investment. No matter whom you give it to, it returns great dividends. –AGE 67

I've learned that making a living is not the same thing as making a life. –AGE 58

• • •

I've learned that if you put a June bug down a girl's dress, she goes crazy. –AGE 6

• • •

I've learned that you can't please some people, no matter what you do. –AGE 35

• • •

I've learned that regardless of how hot and steamy a relationship is at first, the passion fades and there had better be something else to take its place. –AGE 29

I've learned that it's impossible to take a ten-day vacation without gaining ten pounds. –AGE 55

• • •

I've learned that if you want to get promoted, you must do things that get noticed. –AGE 54

• • •

I've learned that you can tell a lot about a couple's relationship by how tidy each leaves the bathroom for the other one. –AGE 51

• • •

I've learned that people allow themselves to be only as successful as they think they deserve to be. –AGE 50

I've learned that it always makes me feel good
to see my parents holding hands.   –AGE 13

• • •

I've learned that you shouldn't confuse a black
crayon with a Tootsie Roll.   –AGE 10

• • •

I've learned that if you wait until all conditions
are perfect before you act, you'll never act.   –AGE 64

• • •

I've learned that if you like yourself and
who you are, then you'll probably like almost
everyone you meet regardless of who they
are.   –AGE 31

I've learned that you don't miss fighting with your sister until she's left for college. —AGE 14

• • •

I've learned that you either control your attitude or it controls you. —AGE 47

• • •

I've learned that nothing is more precious than a baby's laugh. —AGE 29

• • •

I've learned that regardless of what I've had for supper, I can't resist spooning a little peanut butter out of the jar before going to bed. —AGE 48

I've learned that if there are things about your sweetheart that you don't admire, you will like them even less after you marry him. –AGE 25

• • •

I've learned that it's fun and satisfying to write in my journal the good things that happen to me every day. –AGE 16

• • •

I've learned that the best advice you can give anyone is, "Be kind." –AGE 66

• • •

I've learned that even the happiest people have down days. –AGE 27

The Complete Live and Learn and Pass It On

I've learned that worry is often a substitute for action. –AGE 50

. . .

I've learned that there's no friend like an old friend, no dog like an old dog, and no money like old money. –AGE 74

. . .

I've learned that sometimes I just need to be held. –AGE 36

. . .

I've learned that once a woman decides she wants something, never underestimate her ability to get it. –AGE 34

I've learned that it's OK to be content with what you have, but never with what you are. –AGE 51

• • •

I've learned that a person's greatest need is to feel appreciated. –AGE 45

• • •

I've learned that after you've been your own boss, it's tough to go back to working for someone else. –AGE 58

• • •

I've learned that I am quick to count others' offenses against me, but seldom think about what others suffer because of me. –AGE 39

I've learned that whnever you need to borrow
money, it's best to look prosperous. –AGE 49

I've learned that releasing a big fish is more satisfying than eating it. –AGE 42

• • •

I've learned that you always find time to do the things you really want to do. –AGE 64

• • •

I've learned that I would like to be a horse and live on a ranch, if only cowboys didn't wear spurs. –AGE 8

• • •

I've learned that there are people who love you dearly but just don't know how to show it.
–AGE 41

I've learned that you shouldn't confuse
success with usefulness. —AGE 51

. . .

I've learned that regardless of how little
you have, you can always give comfort and
encouragement. —AGE 64

. . .

I've learned that the time I really need a
vacation is when I'm just back from one. —AGE 38

. . .

I've learned that if you give a pig and a boy
everything they want, you'll get a good pig
and a bad boy. —AGE 77

I've learned that you should fill your life with experiences, not excuses. —AGE 51

. . .

I've learned that the greatest risk is in thinking too small. —AGE 61

. . .

I've learned that joy is often the ability to be happy in small ways. —AGE 72

. . .

I've learned that people will obey almost any reasonable request except, "Please remain seated until the captain has brought the aircraft to a complete stop at the gate." —AGE 51

I've learned that a good feeling gets even better when it's shared. —AGE 14

. . .

I've learned that you can make a dime dishonestly, but that it will cost you a dollar later on. —AGE 59

. . .

I've learned that you can have a fancy education and still not be very wise. —AGE 69

. . .

I've learned that it is impossible to accomplish anything worthwhile without the help of other people. —AGE 82

I've learned that a clean car drives better than a dirty one. –AGE 55

· · ·

I've learned that love can break your heart, but it's worth it. –AGE 26

· · ·

I've learned that when traveling the interstates in Ohio, it's best to observe the speed limit.
–AGE 41

· · ·

I've learned that when you're feeling down, brush your teeth. It makes you feel like a fresh new person. –AGE 14

I've learned that I like my teacher because
she cries when we sing "Silent Night."
–AGE 7

• • •

I've learned that Cokes taste better in the
small bottles. –AGE 54

• • •

I've learned that you should make the money
before you spend it. –AGE 48

• • •

I've learned that all women love to get flowers,
especially when there's no particular reason.
–AGE 33

I've learned that learning to forgive takes practice. –AGE 15

• • •

I've learned that heroes are the people who do what has to be done when it needs to be done, regardless of the consequences. –AGE 77

• • •

I've learned that people don't want advice, but understanding. –AGE 40

• • •

I've learned that there comes a time when you must stop grieving over the death of a loved one and get on with your life. –AGE 67

The Complete Live and Learn and Pass It On

I've learned that it's better to be decisive, even if it means I'll sometimes be wrong. –AGE 51

• • •

I've learned that being a good mother is the best occupation you can ever have. –AGE 35

• • •

I've learned that if there were ten people in a hayloft, I'd be the first to jump off. –AGE 13

• • •

I've learned that the secret of success in business is surprisingly simple: give people more than they expect and do it cheerfully.
–AGE 73

I've learned that what sounds like music
to my teenagers sounds like a train wreck
to me. –AGE 44

• • •

I've learned that fourteen days is too long to
spend on an ocean cruise. –AGE 49

• • •

I've learned that it's better not to wait for a
crisis to discover what's important in your life.
–AGE 45

• • •

I've learned that you should never play for a
tie score. Go for the win. –AGE 41

I've learned that when the light turns green, you had better look both ways before proceeding. −AGE 33

• • •

I've learned that the purpose of criticism is to help, not to humiliate. −AGE 49

• • •

I've learned that "call waiting" deserves to be included among the planet's greatest abominations. −AGE 55

• • •

I've learned that nothing very bad or very good ever lasts very long. −AGE 66

I've learned that failures always blame someone else. —AGE 62

• • •

I've learned that old women can get away with anything. —AGE 40

• • •

I've learned that you should treasure your children for what they are, not for what you want them to be. —AGE 39

• • •

I've learned that when I mentally list all the little joys the day has brought me before I fall asleep, I rarely have a sleepless night. —AGE 44

I've learned that there is nothing more peaceful than a sleeping child. —AGE 30

. . .

I've learned that a happy marriage multiplies joys and divides grief. —AGE 79

. . .

I've learned that the important thing is not what others think of me, but what I think of me. —AGE 38

. . .

I've learned that you shouldn't discuss your success with people less successful than you. —AGE 50

I've learned that if you go to a garage sale, you'll almost always buy at least one item you don't need. —AGE 52

. . .

I've learned that women adapt to harsh conditions better and faster than men. —AGE 51

. . .

I've learned that a pat on the back and a sincere "You're doing a great job" can make someone's day. —AGE 49

. . .

I've learned that my worst decisions were made when I was angry. —AGE 62

The Complete Live and Learn and Pass It On

I've learned that bigger is not always better, and that going faster is not necessarily progress. –AGE 73

• • •

I've learned that what some consider genius is often nothing more than good luck. –AGE 59

• • •

I've learned that you can always get more money, but you can never get more time. –AGE 65

• • •

I've learned that you often take out your frustrations on the people you love the most.
–AGE 29

I've learned that as long as you keep music in your life, you'll never need a psychiatrist.

—AGE 17

The Complete Live and Learn and Pass It On

I've learned that the song is right: love is lovelier the second time around. —AGE 34

. . .

I've learned that when people aim for what they want out of life, most aim too low. —AGE 75

. . .

I've learned that you can tell a lot about a man by the happiness of his wife and the respect given him by his children. —AGE 51

. . .

I've learned that marriages are meant to last a lifetime. When they don't, all the world suffers. —AGE 59

I've learned that it is very satisfying to work hard at work that's worth doing. —AGE 52

• • •

I've learned that no man is a match for a woman's tears. —AGE 49

• • •

I've learned that it's easy to go from the simple life to the fast track, but almost impossible to go back the other way. —AGE 44

• • •

I've learned that when I'm given a choice of 31 flavors of ice cream, I still choose vanilla.

—AGE 41

I've learned that milk helps to keep your bones from bending over. −AGE 7

• • •

I've learned that if love isn't taught in the home it's difficult to learn it anywhere else. −AGE 51

• • •

I've learned that no one is ever so powerful or successful that they don't appreciate a sincere compliment. −AGE 62

• • •

I've learned that hatred is like acid. It destroys the vessel that holds it. −AGE 56

I've learned that the best way to attend to any problem is to hurry slowly. –AGE 68

• • •

I've learned that plotting revenge only allows the people who hurt you to hurt you longer.
–AGE 40

• • •

I've learned that there are still some things I haven't made up my mind about yet. –AGE 91

• • •

I've learned that if you stick a piece of ice down a boy's pants, he screams bloody murder. –AGE 10

The Complete Live and Learn and Pass It On

I've learned that even the most mundane job holds the potential for great achievement.
–AGE 53

• • •

I've learned that I am happy when I'm kind to others and unhappy when I'm not. –AGE 88

• • •

I've learned that a woman would rather be complimented about her intelligence than her looks. –AGE 39

• • •

I've learned that enthusiasm and success just seem to go together. –AGE 44

I've learned that my teacher always calls on me the one time I don't know the answer.

–AGE 9

• • •

I've learned that most people resist change, and yet it's the only thing that brings progress.

–AGE 66

• • •

I've learned that to trap mice, peanut butter works better than cheese. –AGE 36

• • •

I've learned not to waste time worrying about the things I can't change. –AGE 72

I've learned that you can love someone and still not like him very much. −AGE 26

. . .

I've learned that meeting interesting people depends less on where you go than on who you are. −AGE 51

. . .

I've learned that regrets over yesterday and the fear of tomorrow are twin thieves that rob us of the moment. −AGE 29

. . .

I've learned that you can never have too many smart people in your life. −AGE 48

I've learned that you never get rewarded for the things you intended to do. —AGE 76

• • •

I've learned a marriage can survive almost anything except the husband staying home all day. —AGE 58

• • •

I've learned that you shouldn't expect life's very best if you're not giving it your very best. —AGE 51

• • •

I've learned that the only time I want to sleep late is when I can't. —AGE 29

I've learned that if you ask someone, "I wonder if you could please help me?" you will almost always get a positive response.   –AGE 57

• • •

I've learned that the trick is to live a long time without growing old.   –AGE 73

• • •

I've learned that you form a committee to "study the matter" when you really don't want to do anything.   –AGE 43

• • •

I've learned that my dog is the only one who knows how to keep his mouth shut.   –AGE 19

I've learned that I still can't eat an Oreo without first opening it up and licking off the filling. —AGE 51

• • •

I've learned that comfortable shoes are a must. —AGE 33

• • •

I've learned that you can tell how good a parent you were by observing your children with their children. —AGE 82

• • •

I've learned that kids need hugs more than they need things. —AGE 43

I've learned that if your teenager doesn't think you're a real embarrassment and a hard-nosed bore, you're probably not doing your job as a parent. —AGE 44

• • •

I've learned that you shouldn't do all your banking at one bank. —AGE 52

• • •

I've learned that the smart husband knows that the wooing never stops. —AGE 59

• • •

I've learned that everybody likes to be asked his or her opinion. —AGE 71

I've learned that when someone gives you free tickets, don't complain about the show.   –AGE 45

• • •

I've learned that whatever I love to do, I do well.   –AGE 48

• • •

I've learned that the higher up you go in a corporation, the nicer the people are and the better manners they have.   –AGE 55

• • •

I've learned that my best friend is my teddy bear. He never tells my secrets.   –AGE 17

I've learned that I am my child's most important teacher. —AGE 32

• • •

I've learned that if I want the circumstances in my life to change for the better, I must change for the better. —AGE 42

• • •

I've learned that the trip is often more fun than the destination. —AGE 62

• • •

I've learned that if you want to know if you love someone, watch them when they're asleep. —AGE 46

I've learned that it's never too late to improve yourself. —AGE 85

• • •

I've learned that when you have three of your wild friends in the car, the driver freaks. —AGE 9

• • •

I've learned a good deal is a good deal only when it's a good deal for both parties. —AGE 47

• • •

I've learned that when visiting my parents, it takes five seconds to say "hello" but about thirty minutes to say "good-bye." —AGE 48

I've learned that I don't understand women and I never will. —AGE 84

• • •

I've learned that talking about your problems doesn't always help. —AGE 15

• • •

I've learned that fame is written in ice and eventually the sun comes out. —AGE 57

• • •

I've learned that I didn't really feel old until my kids started receiving social security benefits. —AGE 92

I've learned that life is like a blind date. Sometimes you just have to have a little faith. —AGE 23

I've learned to be generous with praise but cautious with promises. –AGE 54

• • •

I've learned that goldfish don't like Jell-O.
–AGE 5

• • •

I've learned that to get the right answer, you have to ask the right question. –AGE 39

• • •

I've learned that a time comes when you would give all you possess to have your grown children young again, if only for one day.
–AGE 60

I've learned that the faults I have now are exactly the ones my parents tried to correct when I was a child. —AGE 40

• • •

I've learned that many people give up just when they are about to achieve success. —AGE 48

• • •

I've learned that the people who say, "Money isn't everything," usually have plenty of it.
—AGE 66

• • •

I've learned that the best way to appreciate something is to be without it for a while. —AGE 14

I've learned that it takes as much time and energy to wish as it does to plan. —AGE 49

. . .

I've learned that there's never a snow day on the day I have a big test. —AGE 12

. . .

I've learned that we grow only when we push ourselves beyond what we already know.
—AGE 53

. . .

I've learned that if you don't feel like being pleasant, courteous, and kind, act that way and the feelings will come. —AGE 38

I've learned that people who have mastered the art of living seem to be guided by an internal compass. They may not always stay on track, but they soon return to the proper course. —AGE 63

• • •

I've learned that my mother sometimes laughs so hard she snorts. —AGE 7

• • •

I've learned that for a happy day, look for something bright and beautiful in nature. Listen for a beautiful sound, speak a kind word to some person, and do something nice for someone without their knowledge. —AGE 85

I've learned that you can never have too many friends.   −AGE 16

• • •

I've learned that when things get easy, it's easy to stop growing.   −AGE 53

• • •

I've learned that when you have a wonderful wife, tell others, but be sure to tell her too.
−AGE 51

• • •

I've learned that people are in such a hurry to get to the "good life" that they often rush right past it.   −AGE 72

I've learned that you shouldn't speak unless you can improve on the silence. —AGE 62

• • •

I've learned that you should say your prayers every night. —AGE 9

• • •

I've learned that if chewing gum has been dropped on the sidewalk within the past 48 hours, my shoes will find it. —AGE 28

• • •

I've learned that the man who says he can do as much at 60 as he could do at 30 wasn't doing very much at 30. —AGE 62

I've learned that money is a lousy means of keeping score. —AGE 71

. . .

I've learned that if you wish to do business with honest people, you must be an honest person. —AGE 55

. . .

I've learned that people can change, so give them the benefit of the doubt. —AGE 14

. . .

I've learned that you have little chance of finding the caring, supportive husband of your dreams in a bar. —AGE 29

I've learned that it's never too late to heal an injured relationship. −AGE 57

• • •

I've learned that the little sayings you learn as a child, such as the Golden Rule, are actually important. −AGE 15

• • •

I've learned never to underestimate the potential and power of the human spirit. −AGE 82

• • •

I've learned that when my wife and I finally get a night out without the kids, we spend most of the time talking about the kids. −AGE 29

I've learned that I've never regretted the nice things I've said about people. —AGE 38

I've learned that you can inherit wealth but never wisdom. —AGE 51

• • •

I've learned that the older I get, the less attention I get. —AGE 6

• • •

I've learned that a good relationship between me and my family, my friends, and my business associates can be boiled down to one word: *respect.* —AGE 56

• • •

I've learned that you shouldn't do anything that wouldn't make your mother proud. —AGE 51

I've learned that about 90 percent of the things that happen to me are good and only about 10 percent are bad. To be happy, I just have to focus on the 90 percent. –AGE 54

• • •

I've learned that no matter how bad it gets, when my child hugs my neck and kisses me and says, "Don't worry, Mom, everything will be OK," I know I'll be able to make it. –AGE 28

• • •

I've learned that kind words and good deeds are eternal. You never know where their influence will end. –AGE 51

I've learned that every day you should reach out and touch someone. People love that human touch—holding hands, a warm hug, or just a friendly pat on the back. –AGE 85

• • •

I've learned to keep looking ahead. There are still so many good books to read, sunsets to see, friends to visit, and old dogs to take walks with. –AGE 86

• • •

I've learned that I still have a lot to learn. –AGE 92

Volume II

I've learned that home is the place where we grumble the most and are loved the best. –AGE 89

• • •

I've learned that I shouldn't get out of the shower to answer the phone. It will stop ringing the minute I get to it. –AGE 53

• • •

I've learned that first graders are the only ones who think it's neat when their teeth fall out. –AGE 25

• • •

I've learned that when the traffic signal light says "walk," I'd better run. –AGE 57

I've learned that drinking a Diet Coke doesn't make up for the candy bar I enjoyed earlier.

–AGE 19

• • •

I've learned that the closest I get to living in the fast lane is when I'm going through the express lane in the supermarket. –AGE 69

• • •

I've learned that getting up early is a problem for me and my mom. –AGE 7

• • •

I've learned that I should never tell my husband bad news on an empty stomach. –AGE 60

I've learned that it makes me happy to see the answering machine light flashing when I get home. –AGE 18

. . .

I've learned that you should never put off saying, "I love you," in any relationship as long as you sincerely mean it. Otherwise, you may spend the rest of your life regretting it. –AGE 19

. . .

I've learned that the importance of fame, fortune, and all other things pales in comparison to the importance of positive personal relationships. –AGE 50

I've learned that I should never have taught
my four-year-old sister how to load and shoot
my BB gun.   –AGE 12

• • •

I've learned that when my house is the messiest
my mother-in-law will drop by.   –AGE 29

• • •

I've learned that loaning money to friends and
relatives causes them to get amnesia.   –AGE 32

• • •

I've learned that when the oil light is on in
your car, you really should put some oil in it!
–AGE 23

I've learned that when I'm acting really stupid and I think that no one's watching, the guy I want to impress is watching. –AGE 13

• • •

I've learned that women will never understand the Three Stooges. –AGE 15

• • •

I've learned that all grandchildren are beautiful, brilliant, and take after their grandparents. –AGE 65

• • •

I've learned that being an elementary teacher is the most noble profession of all. –AGE 19

I've learned that saying "hi" to somebody today can result in a new friend tomorrow.

–AGE 18

• • •

I've learned that old age is not a defeat but a victory, not a punishment but a privilege.

–AGE 79

• • •

I've learned that it is no fun to watch television unless you have the remote control. –AGE 23

• • •

I've learned that good or bad, most things don't last very long. –AGE 32

I've learned that just when I think I know everything, my son will ask me something I don't know or can't possibly explain. –AGE 28

• • •

I've learned that an act of love, no matter how great or small, is always appreciated. –AGE 22

• • •

I've learned that ranch dressing tastes good on anything. –AGE 19

• • •

I've learned that my mom is always right about my boyfriends. –AGE 22

I've learned that the way to grow old gracefully is to keep active. –AGE 82

• • •

I've learned that no matter how old or how experienced you are, you can always learn something from a child. –AGE 20

• • •

I've learned that when planning a project, the shortest pencil is worth more than the longest memory. –AGE 38

• • •

I've learned that middle age is the best time of my life—so far. –AGE 50

I've learned that it's best to ask for what you need from your loved ones and not assume that somehow they'll just know. –AGE 34

• • •

I've learned that if these are supposed to be the best years of my life, I'm in for one bumpy ride. –AGE 16

• • •

I've learned that you should never buy white carpet if you have a black dog. –AGE 30

• • •

I've learned that there are two words that will always draw a crowd: Free Food. –AGE 82

I've learned that my husband's encouragement can make me do things I thought I couldn't.

–AGE 32

• • •

I've learned that girls who won't hold frogs, snakes, and mice because it's not a girlish thing to do are missing something good. –AGE 17

• • •

I've learned that you should never lend your brother your allowance. –AGE 11

• • •

I've learned that a handmade quilt gives comfort as well as warmth. –AGE 46

I've learned that no situation is so bad that losing your temper won't make it worse. −AGE 71

• • •

I've learned that you should always put on a new bathing suit and get it wet before wearing it in public. −AGE 21

• • •

I've learned that most people don't look for the truths of life, they only search for someone to agree with them. −AGE 27

• • •

I've learned that everybody wants to be special to someone. −AGE 22

I've learned that my best friend and I can do anything or nothing and have the best time.

–AGE 18

• • •

I've learned that no matter how beautiful your makeup is, it can't hide the expression of a sad heart.   –AGE 21

• • •

I've learned that one sincere apology is worth more than all the roses money can buy.   –AGE 40

• • •

I've learned that of all the bad four-letter words, DIET is the worst.   –AGE 54

I've learned that if you have several tasks, do the hardest one first. Then the rest are a snap.
–AGE 86

• • •

I've learned that you can't believe everything you hear, even if you hear it twice. –AGE 18

• • •

I've learned that you'll never see a U-Haul trailer behind a hearse. –AGE 59

• • •

I've learned that a woman can stand anything but being forgotten or not being needed.
–AGE 89

I've learned that having five brothers and one sister is really a great blessing, even though it has taken me sixteen years to figure out it was a blessing. —AGE 16

• • •

I've learned that country music can always make me feel better when I'm melancholy because the people in the songs are always in a worse situation than I am. —AGE 14

• • •

I've learned that people can surprise you. Sometimes the people you expect to kick you when you're down will be the ones to help you get back up. —AGE 32

I've learned that warmth, kindness, and friendship are the most yearned for commodities in the world. The person who can provide them will never be lonely. –AGE 79

• • •

I've learned that if you leave clothes in the ironing pile long enough, you'll outgrow them and you can sell them at a yard sale.
–AGE 57

• • •

I've learned that you should never tell a child that his dreams are unlikely or outlandish. Few things are more humiliating, and what a tragedy it would be if he believed it. –AGE 18

I've learned that although I can skip class without getting in trouble, there's still the consequence at exam time. –AGE 19

• • •

I've learned that picking out a lunch box for an eight-year-old is a major decision. –AGE 30

• • •

I've learned that if you throw ten socks in the laundry, only nine will come out. –AGE 27

• • •

I've learned that it is never too late to start reading the Bible. –AGE 34

I've learned that a minute of extra thinking beforehand can save hours of worry later.

–AGE 22

. . .

I've learned that all the advice and wisdom in the world cannot help you unless you apply it daily in your life. –AGE 23

. . .

I've learned that the greatest physician in the world is optimism. –AGE 41

. . .

I've learned that there are good neighbors wherever you live. –AGE 30

I've learned that a smile, a "How are you?" and a warm, close, caring hug always give love, faith, and hope. –AGE 54

• • •

I've learned that nothing feels as good as my fiancé's arms around me when we've been separated too long. –AGE 19

• • •

I've learned that good habits are just as hard to break as bad habits. –AGE 62

• • •

I've learned that the easiest way to find happiness is to quit complaining. –AGE 19

I've learned that the prayer I say most often is, "Lord, please keep your arm around my shoulder and your hand over my mouth."

-AGE 34

• • •

I've learned that if you are in a relationship with someone who doesn't believe in you, you should get out before you stop believing in yourself. -AGE 22

• • •

I've learned that it doesn't make any difference whether or not you name your cat. He never comes when called anyway.

-AGE 31

I've learned that when you have problems operating your VCR or DVD, call in your five-year-old grandson. −AGE 73

. . .

I've learned that you are never too old to try something new. −AGE 82

. . .

I've learned that no matter how much a friend promises not to tell anyone else, she always does. −AGE 16

. . .

I've learned that you can't scramble eggs in the toaster oven. −AGE 14

I've learned that I am the only one in my house who cleans the hair out of the shower drain. –AGE 23

• • •

I've learned that when I surprise an old friend with a phone call, it seems like just yesterday that we last spoke. –AGE 38

• • •

I've learned that an adult is someone who stopped growing, except in the middle. –AGE 72

• • •

I've learned that grandmothers are still girls at heart. They like pats, hugs, and kisses. –AGE 85

I've learned that people place too much importance on progress and not enough on maintenance. –AGE 32

. . .

I've learned that the longer you have been in the car with your children, the harder it is to laugh at the jokes they tell. –AGE 33

. . .

I've learned not to slide down wooden stairs with my sled. –AGE 7

. . .

I've learned that whining doesn't solve problems. –AGE 10

I've learned that no matter how closely I follow her recipe, my cooking never tastes as good as my mom's. —AGE 24

I've learned that life is like a ten-speed bicycle. Most of us have gears we never use.

–AGE 59

• • •

I've learned that you shouldn't leave your fork on your plate when you reheat your food in the microwave. –AGE 13

• • •

I've learned that some people love talking about history, especially their own. –AGE 64

• • •

I've learned that I am grateful for what I've learned, no matter what it cost me. –AGE 34

I've learned that when my dog or my children are feeling very insecure, they follow me everywhere—including into the bathroom.

–AGE 42

• • •

I would rather have a best friend than a boyfriend, except maybe on a Friday night.

–AGE 20

• • •

I've learned that you are not an adult until you accept responsibility for your own actions and quit blaming everything on the way your parents reared you.   –AGE 37

I've learned that playing football in the house isn't a good idea.   −AGE 9

• • •

I've learned that whatever color you like the least, your mother-in-law will love the most.
−AGE 33

• • •

I've learned that no one ever drinks the last sip of anything in a container they would have to wash or refill.   −AGE 49

• • •

I've learned that there is no joy like the joy of seeing a child learn to read.   −AGE 18

I've learned that you should keep an open mind, but not so open that your brains fall out.

–AGE 54

• • •

I've learned that absent-minded people get lots of exercise looking for things they can't find. –AGE 66

• • •

I've learned that doctors deserve and appreciate thank-you notes. –AGE 21

• • •

I've learned that good quality underwear is worth the extra cost. –AGE 25

I've learned that sometimes life hands you situations when all you can do is put one foot in front of the other and live moment to moment.   –AGE 66

• • •

I've learned that if you're not willing to move mountains for your friends, they won't be willing to move them for you.   –AGE 18

• • •

I've learned that nothing makes your heart rejoice more than children, all ages and colors, playing happily together on a playground at recess.   –AGE 19

I've learned that life with my husband's faults is hands down better than life without my husband. —AGE 49

• • •

I've learned that you should assemble a baby crib in the room where you intend to use it. It won't fit through the door fully assembled.
—AGE 35

• • •

I've learned that just because someone doesn't love you the way you want them to doesn't mean they don't love you with all they have. —AGE 32

I've learned that taking a break in the middle of a job is not half as relaxing as taking a break after the job is finished. —AGE 16

• • •

I've learned that the best place to fill the sugar bowl is over the sink. —AGE 78

• • •

I've learned that I'm getting more and more like my mom, and I'm kind of happy about it. —AGE 19

• • •

I've learned that you can gain two pounds by eating half a pound of fudge. —AGE 16

I've learned that sometimes when I'm angry
I have the right to be angry, but that doesn't
give me the right to be cruel. –AGE 42

• • •

I've learned that you should hope and work,
but never hope more than you work. –AGE 59

• • •

I've learned that if you finish the toilet paper
roll without replacing it, you will be the first
person who needs it next. –AGE 18

• • •

I've learned that not everyone can be silly.
Some people just don't know how. –AGE 35

I've learned that the best part of the day is when my daughters first get home from school and we talk about their day. –AGE 34

• • •

I've learned that you're asking for trouble when you leave a three-year-old in the car with the keys in the ignition. –AGE 33

• • •

I've learned that true friendship continues to grow, even over the longest distance. –AGE 19

• • •

I've learned that some people can spend years putting off a ten-minute job. –AGE 16

I've learned that I can tell a lot about people by what items they notice in my home. —AGE 45

• • •

I've learned that my mom was right about life when she commented, "No one ever said it would be easy." —AGE 30

• • •

I've learned that nothing will help you stick to a diet more than people telling you how good you are looking. —AGE 23

• • •

I've learned that a mother is only as happy as her child. —AGE 49

I've learned that perspective is everything. To a worm, digging in the hard ground is more relaxing than going fishing. −AGE 65

• • •

I've learned that you shouldn't eat in a restaurant where the cook is skinny. −AGE 55

• • •

I've learned that nothing in the world looks as precious as a sleeping child. −AGE 34

• • •

I've learned that the best way to learn something is to teach it to someone else.
−AGE 20

I've learned that putting toothpaste on your zits will make them go away. –AGE 18

• • •

I've learned that one of the best things I can give a grieving friend is my presence, not my words. –AGE 38

• • •

I've learned that my wife contributes to everything I do simply through being there. –AGE 53

• • •

I've learned that picking out a Halloween pumpkin is fun at any age. –AGE 26

I've learned that the best and most neglected advice I received was from my mother. —AGE 22

• • •

I've learned that there is a great feeling of satisfaction in checking off the final item on my "Things to do today" list. —AGE 34

• • •

I've learned that stain-resistant carpet will stain. —AGE 10

• • •

I've learned that while progress means change, change doesn't always mean progress. —AGE 75

172

I've learned that no matter how long it is between visits, when I see my sisters it's like it has been only a week, not years. –AGE 45

. . .

I've learned that when you have an older brother who is much larger than you, he is always right. –AGE 15

. . .

I've learned that it is easy to meet interesting people in bookstores. –AGE 54

. . .

I've learned that it's worth fighting for causes, but not with people. –AGE 40

I've learned that a kindness given to one person is contagious and will be passed along. —AGE 50

· · ·

I've learned that two retired people cannot live in harmony with a single-control electric blanket. —AGE 68

· · ·

I've learned that when packing for a vacation, you should take half as many clothes as you think you will need and twice as much money. Your clothes and money should run out at about the same time! —AGE 55

I've learned that if you keep your husband's coffee cup filled as you travel, you will never have to ask to stop at a rest area. –AGE 50

• • •

I've learned that a good friend is the one who tells you how you really look in your jeans.
–AGE 25

• • •

I've learned that I appreciate my mother a lot more since I became a mother. –AGE 31

• • •

I've learned that both a young child and an old person can make me feel young. –AGE 48

I've learned that the less time I have to work with, the more things I get done. —AGE 19

• • •

I've learned that having a young friend when you are old is a special joy. —AGE 83

• • •

I've learned that many of my regrets result from things I didn't do. So now I'm more likely to say, "Why not?" instead of "No way." —AGE 53

• • •

I've learned that no matter how much I care, some people just don't care back. —AGE 18

I've learned that you can sit and worry until you are physically ill, but worrying doesn't change things—action does. —AGE 46

I've learned that no matter how old I am, I want my mother when I'm hurting. —AGE 31

. . .

I've learned that if you die broke, the timing was right. —AGE 64

. . .

I've learned that you shouldn't hold important conversations in bathrooms. You never know who is in the next stall. —AGE 14

. . .

I've learned that it is best to give advice in only two circumstances: when it is requested and when it is a life-threatening situation. —AGE 61

I've learned that putting things in a safe place doesn't mean you can find them again when you look. –AGE 58

• • •

I've learned that Santa Claus has good years and bad years. –AGE 10

• • •

I've learned that sending my mother flowers on my birthday with a card saying "Happy Birthday with Love" makes her happy. –AGE 40

• • •

I've learned that you should never go up a ladder with just one nail. –AGE 63

I've learned that marriage is not always easy. You have to work on it more than anything else in life in order to make it successful. –AGE 26

• • •

I've learned that when you buy a musical instrument, never attempt to economize. Buy the best you can afford from a reputable dealer. A cheap instrument will never express the music that is in your heart. –AGE 39

• • •

I've learned that a happy journey almost always depends on choosing the right traveling companion. –AGE 65

I've learned that I was part of the mess. Both my children are gone, and there are still crumbs on the kitchen counter and floor. —AGE 44

• • •

I've learned that we spend too much time wishing for things we don't have and missing the things we do. —AGE 15

• • •

I've learned that maturity has more to do with the types of experiences you've had and what you've learned from them and less to do with how many birthdays you've celebrated.

—AGE 27

I've learned that it's hard to kiss when you are smiling.   —AGE 59

•   •   •

I've learned that an afternoon in my garden is better than an afternoon with a therapist.

—AGE 37

•   •   •

I've learned that you should never be a passenger on a one-seat bicycle.   —AGE 17

•   •   •

I've learned that after winning an argument with my wife, the first thing I should do is apologize.   —AGE 52

I've learned that doing something as a volunteer makes you feel better than if you were paid to do it. –AGE 16

• • •

I've learned that a warm smile beams, "Welcome to this moment." –AGE 50

• • •

I've learned that everyone wants to live on top of the mountain, but all the happiness and growth occurs while you're climbing it. –AGE 57

• • •

I've learned that children more often follow examples and not advice. –AGE 62

I've learned that the love that accompanies the birth of a child exceeds your greatest expectations. —AGE 27

• • •

I've learned that your family sometimes won't be there for you. It may seem funny, but other people you're not even related to can take care of you and love you and teach you to trust people again. Families aren't only biological. —AGE 25

• • •

I've learned that the greatest test of friendship is to take a vacation together and still like each other when you return. —AGE 59

I've learned that although no one admits to liking to have their picture taken, everyone really does. –AGE 32

• • •

I've learned that when writing letters to family and friends, if I put a quote, verse, or poem on the outside of the envelope, it's like sending a warm hug through the mail. –AGE 50

• • •

I've learned that it's a very bad idea to telephone someone when you are angry with him. You should always wait until the next day—always. –AGE 18

I've learned that having a child late in life can be the best thing that ever happened to you.
–AGE 48

• • •

I've learned that no matter how hard I try, chocolate chip cookie dough never makes it to the oven. –AGE 24

• • •

I've learned that you have to listen to your brain. It has lots of information. –AGE 7

• • •

I've learned that nothing makes me feel prettier than when a guy holds the door for me. –AGE 15

I've learned that at age twenty I had no brains but a nice body and at thirty I had brains and too much body. –AGE 34

• • •

I've learned that a homemade banana cream pie will impress a man more than a new dress and a fancy hairdo. –AGE 44

• • •

I've learned that those who reach their goals too easily have aimed too low. –AGE 73

• • •

I've learned that there is no honesty like the honesty of a young child. –AGE 23

I've learned that you should stop asking people for what they cannot give you and be content with what they can give. –AGE 35

• • •

I've learned that you should never take out your teeth when flushing the commode. –AGE 72

• • •

I've learned that your grandparents are always happy to see you, but they are even happier to see you go home. –AGE 12

• • •

I've learned that a peacock today may be a feather duster tomorrow. –AGE 62

I've learned that a mother never really leaves her children at home, even when she doesn't take them along. —AGE 62

• • •

I've learned that all the advice in the world doesn't help some situations. There are many things we have to figure out on our own. —AGE 24

• • •

I've learned that a compliment is appreciated by everyone, especially my spouse. —AGE 34

• • •

I've learned that it's hard to lie when you are looking into your mother's eyes. —AGE 9

I've learned that nobody wants to know what you're doing until you're doing something that you don't want anyone to know. –AGE 28

• • •

I've learned that when your newly born grandchild holds your little finger in his little fist, you're hooked for life. –AGE 74

• • •

I've learned that to accomplish much is to accomplish a little each day. –AGE 56

• • •

I've learned that you should know what a red button is connected to before pushing it. –AGE 21

The Complete Live and Learn and Pass It On

I've learned that rainy Sundays are great for snuggling, reading, napping, and watching old movies—but not necessarily in that order.
–AGE 44

• • •

I've learned that no matter how good a friend someone is, they're going to disappoint you every once in a while and you must forgive them for that. –AGE 18

• • •

I've learned that in this world, you don't need a multitude of friends. All you really need is just one who will stand by you through thick and thin. –AGE 34

I've learned that I can't choose how I feel, but I can choose what I do about it. −AGE 28

• • •

I've learned that if someone asks, "How are you doing?" it's not necessary to give them a full report. −AGE 65

• • •

I've learned that I never have insomnia when it is time to get up in the morning. −AGE 57

• • •

I've learned that you should never jump off the high diving board when you are wearing a bikini. −AGE 11

I've learned that students paying their own way through college never flunk out. –AGE 55

• • •

I've learned that it is just as wrong to be rude to a child as to an adult. In fact, it may be more unforgivable. –AGE 52

• • •

I've learned that the values you pass on to your children will affect generations. –AGE 60

• • •

I've learned that little children demand more physically and teenagers demand more emotionally. –AGE 40

I've learned that I drive faster when a good song comes on the radio. −AGE 22

. . .

I've learned that you can learn to tap dance at age sixty-four. −AGE 65

. . .

I've learned that you shouldn't judge people too quickly. Sometimes they have a good reason for the way they act. −AGE 20

. . .

I've learned that I wish I could have told my mom that I love her one more time before she passed away. −AGE 49

I've learned that after being on a diet for two weeks, all I lose is fourteen days.   –AGE 60

. . .

I've learned that I shouldn't play with mom's hot glue gun on the dining room table.   –AGE 7

. . .

I've learned that children need smiles and hugs more than they need lectures and instructions.   –AGE 48

. . .

I've learned that every wedding involves at least one argument between the bride and her mother.   –AGE 25

I've learned that girls burp as much as boys.
–AGE 11

• • •

I've learned that I should keep my words soft
and tender, because tomorrow I may have to
eat them.   –AGE 83

• • •

I've learned that when you harbor bitterness,
happiness will dock elsewhere.   –AGE 38

• • •

I've learned that in a college dorm sleeping is
the only way to get some time to yourself.
–AGE 20

I've learned that the best way to eat oatmeal is to feed it to the dog while my parents aren't looking. –AGE 14

• • •

I've learned that men don't know what to do when a woman cries. –AGE 30

• • •

I've learned that my hair always looks good on the day I have an appointment to have it cut. –AGE 25

• • •

I've learned that true happiness is when your newborn sleeps through the night. –AGE 30

I've learned that if either of your parents are angry, don't— and I repeat don't— ask for money. –AGE 10

The Complete Live and Learn and Pass It On

I've learned that when I get close to people who are full of anger, their anger spills over onto me. But when I get close to people who are full of love, their love spills over onto me.

–AGE 57

• • •

I've learned that it is just as much fun at age sixty-five to ride a carousel as it is to ride one at age five.   –AGE 67

• • •

I've learned that there is no better greeting than my dog waiting for me on the front porch, wagging his tail.   –AGE 18

I've learned that if I really want that last piece of pie, I should take it. –AGE 62

• • •

I've learned that you shouldn't waste too much of today worrying about yesterday. –AGE 45

• • •

I've learned that no matter how much I complain about it, my husband's snoring is a sound of security. –AGE 21

• • •

I've learned that you don't know the value of a dollar until you've earned it yourself. –AGE 17

I've learned that getting in the kitchen and cooking a healthy meal with the radio on relaxes me at the end of a stressful day. —AGE 36

• • •

I've learned that you should never change everything in your life at once. Keep some things the same just for stability so that it's easier to remember who you are. —AGE 40

• • •

I've learned that nothing beats the taste of a slab of your own homemade bread fresh from the oven, slathered with a spoonful of your own homemade jam. —AGE 67

I've learned that you shouldn't marry a man simply because the rest of your family is in love with him.   –AGE 31

• • •

I've learned that while mileage wears out my automobile, walking three miles a day keeps my body in shape.   –AGE 70

• • •

I've learned that life is tough, but I'm tougher.
–AGE 39

• • •

I've learned that if you pray for your enemies, you will stop hating them.   –AGE 74

I've learned that opportunities are never lost; someone will take the one you miss. –AGE 89

• • •

I've learned that when my desk is clean and organized, I can't find anything. –AGE 20

• • •

I've learned that some people go for brains and some for beauty, but everyone appreciates a good sense of humor. –AGE 30

• • •

I've learned that there's nothing sweeter than sleeping with your babies and feeling their breath on your cheeks. –AGE 38

I've learned that no one is perfect until you fall in love with him.   –AGE 18

•   •   •

I've learned that I learned more in my college dorm than I did in any classroom.   –AGE 26

•   •   •

I've learned that it gives me great pleasure to describe "the best thing that happened to me today" in my daily journal.   –AGE 72

•   •   •

I've learned that marrying an extrovert when you are an introvert can be good for you.
–AGE 35

204

I've learned that when my child gets upset, he calms down much sooner if I stay calm. —AGE 33

• • •

I've learned that what matters is not that you be the best, but that you try your best. —AGE 15

• • •

I've learned that even if you've never had a pimple on the end of your nose before, one will show up there a week before the prom. —AGE 17

• • •

I've learned that regardless of the airport, the shuttle bus for your rental car company is always the last to arrive —AGE 51

I've learned that everyone you meet deserves that first smile. —AGE 23

• • •

I've learned that men would rather be lost for hours than stop and ask for directions. —AGE 30

• • •

I've learned that the patience and love you show your children will surface when they reach the age of thirty. —AGE 63

• • •

I've learned that you can have the most interesting conversations while having your teeth cleaned. —AGE 18

I've learned that people love to get letters from friends and family, no matter what the subject is or the length of the letters. –AGE 22

• • •

I've learned that the fire of a past love will always burn with a small flame. –AGE 18

• • •

I've learned that I always think of the right thing to say when it's too late. –AGE 30

• • •

I've learned that I like to plant my neighbors' favorite flowers in my flower boxes so that they can see and enjoy them. –AGE 50

I've learned that commercials for feminine products always come on when you are sitting in the living room with men. –AGE 19

• • •

I've learned that one of the best things you can do for your children is introduce them to books. –AGE 30

• • •

I've learned that having good hair is better than having good legs. –AGE 19

• • •

I've learned that love, not time, heals all wounds. –AGE 14

I've learned that it isn't always enough to be forgiven by others. Sometimes you have to learn to forgive yourself. —AGE 20

• • •

I've learned that the easiest way for me to grow as a person is to surround myself with people smarter than I am. —AGE 50

• • •

I've learned that I shouldn't go shopping when I'm depressed. I always buy too much. —AGE 30

• • •

I've learned that the Lord didn't do it all in one day. What makes me think I can? —AGE 46

I've learned that you view other people's children in a whole different light when you have one of your own. –AGE 35

• • •

I've learned that even if you move fifteen hundred miles away, your mother still tells you what to do and you still feel like you have to do it. –AGE 21

• • •

I've learned that people always underestimate my ability, but one thing they should never underestimate is the drive behind my ability.

–AGE 25

I've learned that when I walk into my room at the end of the day, I always feel better if my bed is made. –AGE 21

. . .

I've learned that adding extra spices can't cover those cooking mistakes. –AGE 46

. . .

I've learned that when your phone doesn't ring, you should ring someone else's. –AGE 35

. . .

I've learned that when your wife simply answers, "nothing" when you ask her what's wrong, you're in deep trouble. –AGE 37

I've learned that I get a lump in my throat
every time I think of the day when my
daughter will marry. –AGE 44

• • •

I've learned that when you plan to get even with
someone, you are only allowing the person who
has hurt you to hurt you longer. –AGE 13

• • •

I've learned that I wouldn't feel eighty-five
years old if I didn't look in the mirror. –AGE 85

• • •

I've learned that to ignore the facts does not
change the facts. –AGE 56

I've learned that if you want to remember your wedding anniversary forever, just forget it once. —AGE 59

• • •

I've learned that my mom brags when she gets the TV remote control. —AGE 10

• • •

I've learned that the kind of adults my children are now is directly related to the kind of children I continually told them they were. —AGE 50

• • •

I've learned that after all these years, I still have a crush on my husband. —AGE 28

I've learned that whenever I go to grandma's house, I come home with at least a dollar in change. –AGE 9

• • •

I've learned that when you want a garment to shrink, it won't, and when you don't, it will come out of the dryer and fit your cat! –AGE 40

• • •

I've learned that when my dog does his job, I feel relieved! –AGE 56

• • •

I've learned that it really doesn't hurt a child to go to bed without a bath. –AGE 32

I've learned that a smile is an inexpensive way
to improve your looks. —AGE 17

I've learned that if you're still talking about what you did yesterday, you haven't done much today. —AGE 21

• • •

I've learned that I shouldn't confuse the green tube of Ben-Gay with the green tube of hemorrhoidal ointment. —AGE 50

• • •

I've learned that when your five-year-old lies down on the couch, she's sick. —AGE 37

• • •

I've learned that your "I can" is more important than your "IQ." —AGE 14

I've learned that when my best girlfriend tells me she's angry with her boyfriend and that it's okay if I go out with him, she really doesn't mean it. —AGE 61

• • •

I've learned that when someone gives you something, never say, "You shouldn't have." —AGE 50

• • •

I've learned never to humiliate another person. Always give him an honorable way to back down or out of something and still save face. —AGE 25

I've learned that successful parenting is convincing each of your children that he or she is your favorite. –AGE 57

• • •

I've learned that it's fun to brighten someone's day by surprising her with a plate of homemade chocolate chip cookies. –AGE 20

• • •

I've learned that you shouldn't judge a person unless you have talked to him one-on-one. –AGE 11

• • •

I've learned that your ACT score doesn't predict the rest of your life. –AGE 18

I've learned to gather all the crumbs that life throws my way. They soon form a lovely, sweet slice of treasured memories.   –AGE 92

• • •

I've learned that you don't really know someone until you've been to a casino together.   –AGE 46

• • •

I've learned that dinner rolls bake a lot faster if the oven is turned on.   –AGE 37

• • •

I've learned that if you share your garden, you will be rewarded tenfold.   –AGE 44

I've learned that when I feel down, nothing picks me up like hearing my mom say, "I'm proud of you." —AGE 22

• • •

I've learned that no matter how bad your heart is broken, the world does not stop for your grief. —AGE 21

• • •

I've learned that the janitor is the most important person in the building. —AGE 54

• • •

I've learned that you can say anything you need to say if it is done in kindness. —AGE 47

I've learned that when someone says, "I love you," she's really asking, "Do you love me?"

–AGE 23

• • •

I've learned that if for nothing else, boyfriends are good for squishing those big brown spiders that appear in the bathtub. –AGE 24

• • •

I've learned that when I awake aching in various joints and thinking "Oh, what's the use?" if I get out of bed, don some clothes, splash cold water on my face, put on a little lipstick—I can face the world for another day!

–AGE 86

I've learned that you're never too old to learn something from *Sesame Street*.   –AGE 21

• • •

I've learned that little boys cry more than little girls when getting shots.   –AGE 75

• • •

I've learned that under everyone's hard shell is someone who wants to be appreciated and loved.   –AGE 18

• • •

I've learned that you should never hire a plumber who bites his fingernails or an electrician who has singed eyebrows.   –AGE 72

I've learned that when you have spilled something on yourself, the first person to tell you is the last person you see at the end of the day. –AGE 25

• • •

I've learned that no matter their ages, or how far away they may be, you never stop wanting to keep a protective arm around your children.
–AGE 67

• • •

I've learned that even at the age of forty-nine, you can still feel like a twelve-year-old child when your mother is talking to you.
–AGE 49

I've learned that when I want advice, I call my best friend. When I want sympathy, I call my boyfriend. —AGE 48

• • •

I've learned that you shouldn't let a day pass without making at least one person feel good.
—AGE 26

• • •

I've learned that the size of a house has nothing to do with how happy it is inside. —AGE 22

• • •

I've learned that if you're too busy to do a favor for a friend, you're too busy. —AGE 39

I've learned that if you pretend like you're taking notes, the teacher won't call on you.

–AGE 18

• • •

I've learned that once a relationship is over, if you experienced more smiles than tears, then it wasn't a waste of time.   –AGE 26

• • •

I've learned that money doesn't buy class.

–AGE 44

• • •

I've learned that mothers don't have time to be sick.   –AGE 32

I've learned that the best compliment my children gave me was when they said they would like to have a marriage like me and my husband. —AGE 72

. . .

I've learned that when a friend has had a fight with a spouse, he or she can call them every name in the book, but you had better not or you're in big trouble. —AGE 65

. . .

I've learned that when I can't sleep in the middle of the night, I find great joy in watching my husband and children sleeping peacefully. —AGE 37

I've learned that you need to close the door to your house before you rescue a chipmunk from your cat. —AGE 52

• • •

I've learned that if you cut your meatloaf into pieces, your parents will think you ate some of it. —AGE 11

• • •

I've learned that boys only rub your back to find out if you are wearing a bra. —AGE 11

• • •

I've learned that whenever I'm in a big hurry, the person in front of me isn't. —AGE 29

I've learned that you shouldn't always bail your children out of trouble even though you may want to. –AGE 47

. . .

I've learned that whatever else you like to cook, people will remember your homemade soups and biscuits. –AGE 49

. . .

I've learned that even men love to be romanced once in a while. –AGE 19

. . .

I've learned that little boys cannot move about the house without making car sounds. –AGE 36

I've learned that I don't have a right to complain about something if I had the power to change it and didn't. −AGE 22

. . .

I've learned that we should be glad God doesn't give us everything we ask for. −AGE 18

. . .

I've learned that my grown children remember and treasure the things we did rather than the things we bought. −AGE 65

. . .

I've learned that my older brother does not like me to fold his underwear. −AGE 18

I've learned that it's those small, daily happenings that make life so spectacular. –AGE 21

• • •

I've learned that simple walks with my father around the block on summer nights when I was a child did wonders for me as an adult.
–AGE 18

• • •

I've learned that you should wade in a creek every chance you get. –AGE 40

• • •

I've learned that my children expect as much from me as I expect from them. –AGE 51

I've learned that the thing that gives me the most joy is writing to my eighty-three-year-old sister. —AGE 86

• • •

I've learned that when my parents say, "It doesn't matter what we think, you are the one dating him"—they hate the guy. —AGE 24

• • •

I've learned that I shouldn't weigh myself every day when I'm on a diet. —AGE 21

• • •

I've learned that grandmothers are mothers with a second chance. —AGE 58

I've learned that nothing is really work unless you would rather be doing something else.

−AGE 85

· · ·

I've learned that it doesn't matter how young you are when you get married, as long as it is to the right person. −AGE 22

· · ·

I've learned that you should take a wet washcloth in a Ziploc bag on field trips. −AGE 44

· · ·

I've learned that if you are happy, it is because you put others before yourself. −AGE 86

I've learned that life is like a roll of toilet paper. The closer it gets to the end, the faster it goes. —AGE 66

• • •

I've learned that a lonely place in your heart can be filled by volunteer work. —AGE 54

• • •

I've learned that the way a child enters a house after school tells you how his day was.
—AGE 65

• • •

I've learned that the more mistakes I make, the smarter I get. —AGE 13

I've learned that when my spouse has failed to fulfill my needs, it's highly likely I've also neglected his. –AGE 32

• • •

I've learned that a nap in a hammock on a summer's day is the best sleep ever invented.
–AGE 21

• • •

I've learned that being kind is more important that being right. –AGE 34

• • •

I've learned that words harshly spoken are as difficult to retrieve as feathers in a gale. –AGE 60

I've learned that just because two people argue, it doesn't mean they don't love each other. And just because they don't argue, it doesn't mean they do. —AGE 22

. . .

I've learned that all people have both good and bad traits. The secret of a happy marriage is to concentrate on your spouse's good traits.
—AGE 60

. . .

I've learned that when coming home from college, if your little brother wrestles you to the ground, it's his way of telling you he loves you. —AGE 19

I've learned that older people in my family have a wealth of knowledge to share if I just ask and listen. –AGE 26

• • •

I've learned that no matter how serious your life requires you to be, everyone needs a friend to act goofy with. –AGE 21

• • •

I've learned that you should never say no to a gift from a child. –AGE 54

• • •

I've learned that you should never wear your swimsuit on a two-hour ride in the car. –AGE 9

I've learned that you can never be too good a listener when a friend is in need. −AGE 13

• • •

I've learned that using a dollar's worth of gas to save twenty-five cents on a crosstown purchase is poor economics. −AGE 46

• • •

I've learned that I can always pray for someone when I don't have the strength to help him in some other way. −AGE 76

• • •

I've learned that when my baby thinks he is hungry, it doesn't matter what I think. −AGE 37

I've learned that you should never eat a Butterfinger in front of a hungry dog. —AGE 11

• • •

I've learned that you can kill a cockroach with hairspray. —AGE 19

• • •

I've learned that there's nothing better on a rainy day than soup, television, and a nap on the couch. —AGE 21

• • •

I've learned that a good way to get your house clean is to invite someone over for dinner. —AGE 50

I've learned that our background and circumstances may have influenced who we are, but we are responsible for who we become. —AGE 25

. . .

I've learned that when you are really stressed out, the cure is to put two miniature marshmallows up your nose and try to "snort" them out. —AGE 11

. . .

I've learned that having three teenage sons at the same time in the same household is as close to temporary insanity as I ever want to be. —AGE 39

I've learned that children, no matter what their age, are always hungry when they go to grandma's house. –AGE 25

• • •

I've learned that the best time to go through your brothers' stuff is when they are not at home. –AGE 12

• • •

I've learned that a new baby changes all your priorities. –AGE 28

• • •

I've learned that the best tranquilizer is a clear conscience. –AGE 76

240

I've learned that the best way to succeed is to do small things well. —AGE 68

• • •

I've learned that my wife's cooking is always good, no matter how bad it is. —AGE 31

• • •

I've learned that the best time to ask your dad if you can do something is when he's sleeping. —AGE 11

• • •

I've learned that children sleep better if they have had a hug and a kiss from both mom and dad. —AGE 60

I've learned that there's always room for dessert. —AGE 12

I've learned that nothing beats a hot summer night, a car full of friends, the windows down, music playing, and whistling at boys! –AGE 18

• • •

I've learned that my father saved me from many a foolish act with these words: "Go ask your mother." –AGE 16

• • •

I've learned that it's all worth it when you are doing a sink full of dishes and your eighteen-year-old comes up behind you and gives you a big hug. And you ask, "What was that for?" And she replies, "No special reason." –AGE 42

I've learned that I need to let my friends comfort me and hold me up, to let them know I need support, that I'm not always as strong as I look or act.   –AGE 49

• • •

I've learned that when I'm waiting to see the doctor, I always wish I had stuck to my diet.

–AGE 47

• • •

I've learned that scratches on furniture made when your children were little become fond memories when they are grown and gone.

–AGE 72

I've learned that as soon as you get rid of something you haven't used in years, you need it the very next week. –AGE 38

• • •

I've learned that what we have done for ourselves alone dies with us. What we have done for others and the world remains and is immortal. –AGE 89

• • •

I've learned that although I didn't understand the principles of gravity in high school physics, I do now when I look at my fifty-year-old body. –AGE 50

I've learned that sometimes when my friends divorce, I'm forced to choose sides even when I don't want to. —AGE 44

. . .

I've learned that you should always accept a foreign exchange student into your home if given the chance. —AGE 37

. . .

I've learned that I should not eat jalapeños the night before traveling. —AGE 37

. . .

I've learned that there is nothing like the feel of warm mud between your toes. —AGE 22

I've learned that sometimes all a person needs is a hand to hold and a heart to understand. −AGE 19

• • •

I've learned that when I go to a cafeteria, I always eat too much. −AGE 38

• • •

I've learned that a loving, faithful wife is a man's greatest treasure. −AGE 68

• • •

I've learned that if you wouldn't write it down and sign it, you probably shouldn't say it.
−AGE 21

I've learned that people will remember you as being a great conversationalist if you mostly listen. −AGE 49

* * *

I've learned that there is a great feeling of independence when you buy your first silverware. −AGE 72

* * *

I've learned that just one person saying to me, "You've made my day!" makes my day. −AGE 20

* * *

I've learned that flipping through the channels is not annoying if I hold the remote. −AGE 42

I've learned that having a child fall asleep in your arms is one of the most peaceful feelings in the world. —AGE 22

• • •

I've learned that having a party when your parents are out of town is taking a great risk. —AGE 15

• • •

I've learned that I should never let my little brother take me for a ride in the golf cart. —AGE 11

• • •

I've learned that life is too short not to do it right the first time. —AGE 82

I've learned that the best classroom in the world is at the feet of an elderly person.

–AGE 47

• • •

I've learned that I shouldn't write anything in a letter that I wouldn't want printed on the front page of a newspaper.   –AGE 67

• • •

I've learned that if you want to go to parties, you have to give some parties.   –AGE 38

• • •

I've learned that no one can keep a secret.

–AGE 17

250

I've learned that I feel better about myself when I make others feel better about themselves. −AGE 18

• • •

I've learned that there is a great thrill in making pickles and jellies with the same friend I used to make mud pies with. −AGE 60

• • •

I've learned that being quiet doesn't always mean you have nothing to say. −AGE 17

• • •

I've learned that when you're in love, it shows.
−AGE 28

I've learned that there is nothing more soothing than the sound of a piano on a sunny Sunday morning. –AGE 32

• • •

I've learned that whenever my mom calls me on the phone to say "hi," it always makes me smile. –AGE 20

• • •

I've learned that a kindness done is never lost. It may take a while, but like a suitcase on a luggage carousel, it will return again. –AGE 77

Volume III

I've learned that you realize you have locked the keys in your car the instant you slam the door shut. —AGE 44

• • •

I've learned that a car only feels new until you make the first payment. —AGE 16

• • •

I've learned that if you're going to pray about something, why worry? If you're going to worry, why pray? —AGE 70

• • •

I've learned that a hug from my husband sends his strength into my body. —AGE 39

I've learned that children do not want anything until after you have poured milk into your cereal. –AGE 19

• • •

I've learned that you shouldn't choose a roommate who comes to look at the place with her boyfriend. –AGE 23

• • •

I've learned that you should never be too busy to say "please" and "thank you." –AGE 36

• • •

I've learned that you can't be a hero without taking chances. –AGE 43

I've learned that I've never regretted doing extra work. −AGE 17

• • •

I've learned that if Mom's on a diet, everyone's on a diet. −AGE 10

• • •

I've learned that the small garden tools I can't find will be in plain sight as soon as I purchase new ones. −AGE 63

• • •

I've learned that you should never give your wife an ironing board for Christmas even if she says she needs a new one. −AGE 39

I've learned that you should never attempt putting on a brand new pair of support hose in 90-degree weather after taking a shower.

–AGE 39

• • •

I've learned that if you have something, material or physical, that gets broken, lost, or damaged, if it can be repaired, replaced, or healed, then you have nothing to worry about.

–AGE 74

• • •

I've learned that when I am feeling terribly unloved by someone, I need to ask myself what I've done recently to love them.   –AGE 29

I've learned that a creative mess is preferable to idle neatness. —AGE 85

. . .

I've learned that when my neighbor's children come over for the day, it makes me appreciate mine all the more. —AGE 25

. . .

I've learned that you should never park your new car beside a beat-up car in the parking lot. —AGE 72

. . .

I've learned that you should get a puppy before you decide to have children. —AGE 28

I've learned that you should never let your wildest, craziest friend put her hand on the back of your head in front of a whipped cream cake. —AGE 8

• • •

I've learned that there's more to life than keeping everything you own, including your person, looking like it's never been used.
—AGE 50

• • •

I've learned that while you hated nap time in pre-school, you would love for your manager to hand you a blanket, a pillow, and a glass of Kool-Aid at work. —AGE 24

I've learned that even with the lights out, I can still find the cashews in the mixed nuts. –AGE 50

• • •

I've learned the great value of the three Fs: Forgive, Forget, and Forge ahead. –AGE 47

• • •

I've learned that you should never eat the cafeteria food when it looks like it's moving.
–AGE 12

• • •

I've learned that the better the doctor, the harder it is to read his or her handwriting.
–AGE 51

I've learned that my dad likes to get those sweet, mushy greeting cards as much as my mom does. —AGE 26

• • •

I've learned that you should never use safety pins while changing a baby's diaper on a waterbed. —AGE 26

• • •

I've learned that a strong code of ethics is as reliable as a compass. —AGE 43

• • •

I've learned that self-pity is a waste of time. —AGE 81

I've learned that I should always laugh at my dad's jokes no matter how lame they are. –AGE 13

• • •

I've learned that it's okay to feel sorry for yourself; just don't let it last for more than five minutes. –AGE 57

• • •

I've learned that a good way to save money is to be too busy to go shopping. –AGE 88

• • •

I've learned that you should never tell your little brother that you're not going to do what your mom told you to do. –AGE 12

I've learned that you should never hit a pile of dog-do with a weed whacker. –AGE 39

. . .

I've learned that when my son is pitching, they all look like strikes to me. –AGE 34

. . .

I've learned that when my husband misplaces one of his belongings, he expects me to know exactly where he left it. –AGE 24

. . .

I've learned that mothers don't always know best. Sometimes they're learning as they go along. –AGE 14

learned that no matter how small the
en, never buy a table with only two
–AGE 42

. . .

ed that the best weight-loss program
heart.   –AGE 24

. . .

at when you tell your younger
can fly, he'll try it.   –AGE 12

. . .

hen you are away at
the mailbox at least twice

I've learned that when you've pushed yourself
as far as you think you can go, you can always
go just a little bit further. –AGE 23

. . .

I've learned that a bottle of catsup should be
on the table three times a day if there is
a child in the house.   –AGE 60

. . .

I've learned that there is no feeling quite so
nice as your child's hand in yours.   –AGE 37

. . .

I've learned that when you're in love, you
always have something to talk about.   –AGE 20

I've learned that you should never be sarcastic with police officers. —AGE 43

I've learned that what I call ... calls messy. —AGE 11

I've learned that t... to sit in the stra... my lap. —AGE

I've ... g...

I've ...
—AGE 46

I've
kitch
chairs

I've learn
is a broker

I've learned t...
brother that he

I've learned that ...
college, you check...
a day. —AGE 18

268

I've learned that to stay away from a previous argument, you need to stay away from the person you're having the argument with.
–AGE 18

. . .

I've learned that you shouldn't ask for anything that costs more than five dollars when your parents are doing taxes.   –AGE 9

. . .

I've learned that you should never leave your one-year-old Dalmatian alone in a room with a black permanent marker and real clean carpet.   –AGE 11

I've learned that the day the bill that you're going to hide arrives will be the day your husband goes to the mailbox first. —AGE 32

• • •

I've learned that nothing smells as good as my boyfriend's favorite sweater. —AGE 19

• • •

I've learned that I know I am growing old when my ballpoint pens are inscribed with the names of companies now defunct. —AGE 71

• • •

I've learned that men who wear boxer shorts are more fun. —AGE 21

I've learned that when your wife asks for a kiss, you shouldn't say, "I already did."
–AGE 67

. . .

I've learned that when your daughter borrows your car, the radio dials are never where you set them. –AGE 47

. . .

I've learned that it takes years to build up trust and only seconds to destroy it. –AGE 15

. . .

I've learned that you should never try to push a pig around that is bigger than you are. –AGE 11

I've learned that when I cook using my grandma's recipes, my kitchen smells as good as hers. —AGE 27

• • •

I've learned that it's best not to discuss how many children I want to have while my wife is pregnant. —AGE 41

• • •

I've learned that living alone after an unhappy marriage is heaven. —AGE 80

• • •

I've learned that I want to exercise, but not now. —AGE 54

I've learned that no matter how many expensive toys you lavish on your cats, they still prefer empty paper sacks! −AGE 24

. . .

I've learned that I can't dust the table with the photo albums on it without stopping to look at the pictures. −AGE 42

. . .

I've learned that wives don't want advice, they mostly just want to be held. −AGE 32

. . .

I've learned that you shouldn't hold a baby above your head after he has eaten. −AGE 14

I've learned that it's not a good idea to try to break in a new bra during a transcontinental flight. –AGE 46

• • •

I've learned that when a father takes a son fishing, the least important thing to either one is whether they catch any fish. –AGE 22

• • • .

I've learned that being a teenager is as hard on your parents as it is on you. –AGE 13

• • •

I've learned that you should be careful when sitting down in a chair that has rollers. –AGE 72

I've learned that working in a garden at sunrise has a tremendous effect on the soul.
–AGE 32

• • •

I've learned that when you're at a family picnic, you shouldn't say you don't like what you're eating because the person sitting next to you might have prepared it.   –AGE 18

• • •

I've learned as a sixth grade teacher that when I send more than two boys to the restroom at a time, the principal usually ends up bringing them back.   –AGE 34

I've learned that we don't have to change friends if we understand that friends change.

–AGE 16

• • •

I've learned that I should listen carefully to any advice my grandparents offer. It is the most valuable advice I can get.   –AGE 20

• • •

I've learned that stopping at third base adds nothing to the score.   –AGE 66

• • •

I've learned that it is okay to give advice but you shouldn't expect anyone to take it.   –AGE 86

I've learned that falling snow is the prettiest when seen through the sunroof of a moving car. –AGE 15

• • •

I've learned that I shouldn't inhale through my nose when I'm eating a powdered doughnut. –AGE 51

• • •

I've learned that a good-looking doctor can make your blood pressure go up. –AGE 43

• • •

I've learned that you should never carry your lunch tray with only one hand. –AGE 9

I've learned that when you buy a car for the first time, your number of friends increases dramatically. –AGE 16

• • •

I've learned that your dog lives with you, but you live with your cat. –AGE 49

• • •

I've learned that you should never underestimate a child's ability to get into more trouble. –AGE 15

• • •

I've learned that biscuits will not brown until you walk away from the oven; then they burn.
–AGE 19

I've learned that a funny hat can change your attitude. —AGE 22

• • •

I've learned that broken cookies have fewer calories. —AGE 82

• • •

I've learned that the side of the milk carton that says "Open Here" is harder to open than the other side. —AGE 54

• • •

I've learned that if my best friend doesn't like my boyfriend, I should look for a new boyfriend. —AGE 20

I've learned that pizza is good for breakfast, lunch, and dinner. –AGE 22

• • •

I've learned that sometimes just taking a nap can be the best medicine. –AGE 18

• • •

I've learned that people have no interest in going into a room until they see that the door is shut. –AGE 23

• • •

I've learned that everyone has two choices—either you grow up and take responsibility for your life or you don't. –AGE 51

I've learned good cooks never lack friends.

–AGE 42

I've learned that I should never write anything in my diary that I wouldn't want someone to read, and that I shouldn't do anything that I wouldn't write in my diary.   —AGE 21

•   •   •

I've learned that as you grow older, everything seems to settle south. Sometimes you are lucky enough to have it be your address as well.   —AGE 39

•   •   •

I've learned that happiness is not how much you have but your capacity to enjoy what you have.   —AGE 44

I've learned that the biggest regrets in life are the risks that you didn't take. –AGE 14

• • •

I've learned that you shouldn't cry over anything that can't cry back. –AGE 60

• • •

I've learned that some folks are like the bottom half of a fraction: The bigger they try to be, the smaller they really are. –AGE 60

• • •

I've learned that child-proof bottles of medicine are sometimes adult-proof, too. –AGE 55

I've learned that cereal always tastes better from the little snack boxes. —AGE 29

* * *

I've learned that as soon as I've cleaned up the kitchen, someone says they're hungry. —AGE 62

* * *

I've learned that maybe someday I'll be as perfect as I say I am when I fill out a job application. —AGE 20

* * *

I've learned that it's easier to be patient with my granddaughter than it was with my own daughters when they were her age. —AGE 53

I've learned that a 6.8 earthquake makes all your other problems seem trivial. —AGE 28

• • •

I've learned that fourteen-year-old sisters take literally a recipe that says "mix by hand." —AGE 18

• • •

I've learned that you should never let a day pass without telling your wife you love her. —AGE 61

• • •

I've learned that reading my son's favorite story book to my grandson is a very pleasurable experience. —AGE 62

I've learned that you should never date a man who is prettier than you are. –AGE 31

• • •

I've learned that if you say "I love you" to your parents, they're going to ask, "What do you want?" –AGE 13

• • •

I've learned that you don't really know a person until you've made them mad. –AGE 22

• • •

I've learned that my mom was right. All those popular, promiscuous girls with the groovy clothes did amount to nothing. –AGE 38

I've learned that wearing anything too small is a sure way to ruin my day. −AGE 44

• • •

I've learned that a great personality can make someone seem to grow more attractive every day. −AGE 20

• • •

I've learned that those who ask "Can you keep a secret?' can't. ·AGE 78

• • •

I've learned that the worst thing in life to be without is love, but toilet paper comes in a close second. −AGE 59

I've learned that no matter how anxious I may seem to send my kids off to school in the morning, nothing makes me happier than seeing them come home in the afternoon.

–AGE 42

• • •

I've learned that you have to reach for the stars. They're not just gonna land on your front porch. –AGE 15

• • •

I've learned that if I think of my husband's snoring as a happy cat purring, I can handle it better for a little while. –AGE 34

I've learned that someone who has never said "I'm sorry" after a five-year relationship is not someone I want to spend the rest of my life with. —AGE 22

• • •

I've learned that the gauge of success is not whether you have a tough problem, but whether it's the same problem you had last year. —AGE 49

• • •

I've learned that the wealthiest of women is she whose daughter grows up to be her best friend. —AGE 74

I've learned that it is impossible to win an argument with a six-year-old. —AGE 18

• • •

I've learned that the more you're in a hurry, the longer it takes to get your school locker open. —AGE 13

• • •

I've learned that the sweetest sound of all is my own name spoken by a boy I care about. —AGE 18

• • •

I've learned that when you go to the dentist, it pays if you've brushed your teeth. —AGE 11

I've learned that no matter how intelligent you are, there is always something to be learned from someone older. –AGE 18

• • •

I've learned that when I'm angry, my mouth works faster than my brain. –AGE 58

• • •

I've learned that praying for your enemies instead of fighting with them helps both them and you. –AGE 14

• • •

I've learned that after you retire, you spend half your time looking for things you lose. –AGE 74

I've learned that to enjoy time alone, you must first appreciate the person you are with. –AGE 51

• • •

I've learned that you should never try to ride your bicycle over a basketball. –AGE 14

• • •

I've learned that if you want an immediate high, give a homeless person ten dollars.
–AGE 32

• • •

I've learned that you can live with choices you have made yourself, but you live to regret the choices you let others make for you. –AGE 29

I've learned that to find the best places in a town to eat, ask a fireman or policeman. —AGE 34

. . .

I've learned that in relationships, it's better to have an end with misery than misery without an end. —AGE 43

. . .

I've learned that if you have a job without any problems, you don't have much of a job. —AGE 35

. . .

I've learned that if you spend your life always looking forward to something else, the present just slips away. —AGE 16

I've learned that you lose only the expensive sunglasses and pens. The cheap ones are always around. –AGE 32

• • •

I've learned that at age 25 you're finding yourself, at age 45 you know yourself, and at age 65 you can be yourself. –AGE 68

• • •

I've learned that anger is an ill wind that blows out the lamp of reason. –AGE 76

• • •

I've learned that you can't raise your family or run a business by remote control. –AGE 45

I've learned that the only thing you can be sure of improving is yourself. —AGE 61

• • •

I've learned that work is when you sweat and you don't want to. Leisure is when you sweat and you don't care. —AGE 55

• • •

I've learned that you should never mention ice cream while you're baby-sitting if you're not sure there's some in the refrigerator. —AGE 11

• • •

I've learned that bragging on your children is one of life's greatest pleasures. —AGE 32

I've learned that there is no advertising as effective as something recommended by a friend. –AGE 39

• • •

I've learned that you can tell a lot about people by looking in the trunk of their car.
–AGE 50

• • •

I've learned that if you have a loving family, it's amazing what you can do without. –AGE 39

• • •

I've learned that when you begin to ask yourself if it's your fault, it usually is. –AGE 20

I've learned that when my older sister says that she'll be out of the bathroom in five minutes, I should just sit down and start reading *War and Peace*. –AGE 14

• • •

I've learned that it's better to hear from your children and grandchildren when they want something than never to hear from them at all.
–AGE 60

• • •

I've learned that the sticky price tags on items purchased at a discount store are always harder to remove than the price tags on items purchased at a prestigious store. –AGE 33

I've learned that a woman who can potty-train triplets can do anything.

–AGE 29

I've learned that the more content I am with myself, the fewer material things I need.

–AGE 36

• • •

I've learned that the most endearing three little words I can say to my wife are, "Let's eat out." –AGE 71

• • •

I've learned that you should never leave home without a sense of humor. –AGE 69

• • •

I've learned that you're never too old to be tucked in. –AGE 19

I've learned that making sure my best friend is happy is as important as making sure that I'm happy. –AGE 19

• • •

I've learned that the word "oops" is not in God's vocabulary. –AGE 32

• • •

I've learned that true friends are the ones who don't put pressure on you to do bad things.
–AGE 11

• • •

I've learned that I cry each time I watch the movie *Father of the Bride*. –AGE 38

I've learned that if I had listened to Mom,
I would have avoided 90 percent of life's
problems. −AGE 20

• • •

I've learned that we are judged by what we
finish, not by what we start. −AGE 62

• • •

I've learned that the friend you've just met can
be a truer friend than the one you've known
all your life. −AGE 19

• • •

I've learned that you should never pull a loose
tooth with tweezers. −AGE 8

I've learned that you get the best feeling when you return home after a long absence and see that everything is just the same as when you left. –AGE 20

•   •   •

I've learned that people tend to rise to accomplishments they thought were beyond them if you show them by your confidence that they can do it. –AGE 53

•   •   •

I've learned that the desire to have a positive impact on the life of each person I meet every day has had an even bigger impact on my life. –AGE 38

I've learned that the easiest way to get grounded is to interrupt my mother during *Seinfeld*. –AGE 17

• • •

I've learned that I can never go to Wal-Mart and buy just one thing. –AGE 24

• • •

I've learned that breaking rules always has consequences, especially when you've broken your own rules. –AGE 16

• • •

I've learned that good advice is no better than poor advice unless you take it. –AGE 58

I've learned that no one was put here to be in charge of making me happy. That's my job.
—AGE 42

• • •

I've learned that every time I call someone that I haven't spoken to in a long time, they say, "I was just going to call you." —AGE 33

• • •

I've learned that you should be grateful for all you have, even if it isn't enough. —AGE 42

• • •

I've learned that the clothes I like best are the ones with the most holes in them. —AGE 26

I've learned that the older my parents get, the sweeter their voices sound. –AGE 34

. . .

I've learned that change is a challenge for the courageous, an opportunity for the alert, and a threat to the insecure. –AGE 87

. . .

I've learned that my cat purrs loudest when he's lying on the book I'm trying to read.
–AGE 22

. . .

I've learned that will power is the ultimate power. –AGE 16

I've learned that the smell of a dentist's office gives me a headache. –AGE 15

• • •

I've learned that big problems are no match for big, brave hearts. –AGE 57

• • •

I've learned that words are the most powerful weapon in the world and should be used with extreme caution. –AGE 52

• • •

I've learned that nothing tastes as sweet as a kiss from a child who's just sucked on a lollipop. –AGE 29

I've learned that the more respect I give my parents, the more respect they give me.

• • •

I've learned that the greatest love always shows up unexpectedly and sometimes in the most uncommon place. –AGE 27

• • •

I've learned that love isn't something you look for, it's something you give. –AGE 36

• • •

I've learned that I should never go in my parents' bedroom on Sunday nights. –AGE 13

I've learned that no matter what ailment you go to the doctor for, it feels better once you get there. –AGE 55

. . .

I've learned that there is a big difference between two cloves of garlic and two bulbs of garlic. –AGE 37

. . .

I've learned that wisdom is not how much you know but how you use what you know. –AGE 57

. . .

I've learned that nothing is impossible for the man who doesn't have to do it himself. –AGE 22

I've learned that the older I get, the more I say "I don't know." When I was younger, I thought I knew it all. –AGE 65

• • •

I've learned that the wealthy person is the one who's content with what he has. –AGE 61

• • •

I've learned that you can miss a lot of good things in life by having the wrong attitude.
–AGE 82

• • •

I've learned that I'm thankful for my parents' boundaries and rules. –AGE 13

I've learned that a shoeshine box made by my eight-year-old son at Vacation Bible School is my most prized possession. –AGE 42

• • •

I've learned that the day you begin a diet, someone wants to take you to dinner in your favorite restaurant. –AGE 24

• • •

I've learned that even God sometimes needs a little time to think things over. –AGE 79

• • •

I've learned that dreams are where you want to go. Work is how you get there. –AGE 20

The Complete Live and Learn and Pass It On

I've learned that it's not what you have in your life but who you have in your life that counts. —AGE 30

I've learned that the best therapy in the world is driving my convertible on a sunny day with no destination in mind.   –AGE 25

• • •

I've learned that when my mom says "We'll talk about it later," the answer is really no.   –AGE 7

• • •

I've learned that you know you're in love when you don't have to ask anyone else if you are.
–AGE 20

• • •

I've learned that if you enjoy being a guest, you must sometimes be a host.   –AGE 41

312

I've learned that nothing is quite as good as the first scoop of peanut butter out of a new jar. –AGE 34

. . .

I've learned that if the one you're with doesn't make you a better and stronger person, you're with the wrong person. –AGE 25

. . .

I've learned that if you want an honest answer about how you look, ask your little sister. –AGE 13

. . .

I've learned that God doesn't ask you to be the best, just to do your best. –AGE 25

I've learned that you can make anyone smile if you give them a box of crayons and a coloring book. –AGE 21

• • •

I've learned that I should never pinch my husband's nostrils together while he's snoring. –AGE 40

• • •

I've learned that you should never walk on ice with your hands in your pockets. –AGE 12

• • •

I've learned that if you do not expect a thank-you, giving is easy. –AGE 47

I've learned that a daughter is never too old to hug and kiss her father in public. –AGE 25

. . .

I've learned that it's discouraging to go swimsuit shopping with someone who wears a size three. –AGE 17

. . .

I've learned that because I have four children, aged 19, 16, 13, and 8, there is no real purpose for the snap on my wallet. –AGE 42

. . .

I've learned that when your grandma says your feet smell a little, they really stink. –AGE 12

I've learned that anything that lasts only a short time is not worth making lifetime sacrifices for. —AGE 25

• • •

I've learned that if you don't want to forget something, stick it in your underwear drawer. —AGE 18

• • •

I've learned that if you tell a girl you love her, she will hit you. —AGE 10

• • •

I've learned that when my response to rudeness is kindness, I feel better. —AGE 62

I've learned that it's embarrassing to have a glamour photograph made of yourself and not have anyone recognize that it's you. –AGE 43

• • •

I've learned that the only thing you do your first year of college is to gain weight. Then you spend the next three years trying to lose it.
–AGE 20

• • •

I've learned that about the only time my boss will return my phone calls is five minutes before I arrive in the morning, five minutes after I leave in the evening, or when I've gone to lunch. –AGE 38

I've learned that you shouldn't be so eager
to find out a secret. It could change your life
forever. –AGE 31

• • •

I've learned that men don't do laundry
because washing machines don't have remote
controls. –AGE 75

• • •

I've learned that anticipation is often better
than the real thing. –AGE 46

• • •

I've learned that animals can sometimes warm
your heart better than people can. –AGE 15

I've learned that the panicky feeling you get when your purse is missing is difficult to surpass. –AGE 62

• • •

I've learned that doing volunteer work is one way for me to repay life for all of the wonderful things that I've been given. –AGE 38

• • •

I've learned that time spent with your kids pays lifetime dividends. –AGE 61

• • •

I've learned that the only surprise a box of cereal holds these days is the price. –AGE 46

I've learned that no matter how old I get, I like my mom taking care of me when I'm sick.
—AGE 25

. . .

I've learned that whenever I leave home without any make-up on, I'll run into my ex-boyfriend. —AGE 26

. . .

I've learned that you shouldn't let anyone apologize to you through a closed door. —AGE 15

. . .

I've learned that good manners are always in style. —AGE 57

I've learned that sticking to my values has not always made the road easy, but it has made me a stronger person for having traveled the harder route. —AGE 30

• • •

I've learned that no matter where I go or where I visit, my favorite place in the whole world is my room. —AGE 15

• • •

I've learned that no matter how much you fight with your siblings during childhood, they grow up to be some of your best friends in your adult life. —AGE 25

I've learned that when your teenager says,
"I hate you," respond by saying, "I love you."
–AGE 44

• • •

I've learned that a diet is the penalty we pay
for exceeding the food limit.   –AGE 76

• • •

I've learned that I can't attend my child's
school performance without a tissue in hand.
–AGE 29

• • •

I've learned that I know I've had a great day if
I come home and my clothes are dirty.   –AGE 19

I've learned that when I want something done around my house, all I have to do is mention to my dad that I'm going to do it myself. –AGE 22

• • •

I've learned that when my dad and I jog together, it strengthens our relationship with each other as well as our bodies. –AGE 18

• • •

I've learned that you leave a little piece of yourself with everyone you teach. –AGE 26

• • •

I've learned that wherever I go, the world's worst drivers have followed me there. –AGE 29

I've learned that when you're worried, give your troubles to God; He will be up all night anyway. –AGE 47

• • •

I've learned that if you're too embarrassed to tell your best friend about something you've done, then you shouldn't have done it in the first place. –AGE 25

• • •

I've learned that saying "Forgive me" is not the hardest thing for some people to say. Saying "You are forgiven" seems to be more difficult. –AGE 70

I've learned that traffic lights and golf balls never do what you tell them to, no matter how much you shout at them. –AGE 43

. . .

I've learned that my car runs better going home. –AGE 92

. . .

I've learned that when a girl keeps on teasing you and says she doesn't like you and bugs you all the time, she really likes you. –AGE 8

. . .

I've learned that I'm the special person I've been saving the good dishes for. –AGE 61

I've learned that two people can look at the same exact thing and see something totally different. −AGE 20

• • •

I've learned that when you say the phrase "I'm not supposed to tell you this but . . . ," you've said too much already. −AGE 19

• • •

I've learned that if you can't fit it in a van, you probably can't fit it in a dorm room. −AGE 18

• • •

I've learned that you're not always perfect on the first try. −AGE 10

I've learned that giving flowers makes me just as happy as receiving them. –AGE 23

• • •

I've learned that if you want peace and quiet, don't buy your four-year-old a whistle—no matter how much he begs. –AGE 43

• • •

I've learned that you should never cut or highlight your own hair. –AGE 28

• • •

I've learned that a well-reared child results in rewarding grandchildren, even to the fourth generation. –AGE 85

I've learned that no matter how hard you try, you can't get ice out of the freezer without dropping at least one cube. –AGE 32

• • •

I've learned that saving is just like dieting: It's never too late to start. –AGE 33

• • •

I've learned that if the peanut butter and jelly don't leak out of the sandwich, there's not enough peanut butter and jelly on it. –AGE 50

• • •

I've learned that it's not a good idea to put bubble bath in a Jacuzzi. –AGE 32

I've learned that
there should be
an Eleventh
Commandment:
Thou shalt not whine.

—AGE 62

I've learned that it is fun when my mom lets me carve my initials in a new jar of peanut butter. –AGE 16

• • •

I've learned that my hair will be perfect on nights I'm home alone and unmanageable when I have a date. –AGE 20

• • •

I've learned that I should never have spent so much time freaking out over my wedding. Everything I was so worried about turned out to be very trivial in the long run. I should have relaxed and enjoyed the moment. –AGE 27

I've learned that you should never tell your fourteen-year-old brother you can beat him up unless you're sure you can. –AGE 21

• • •

I've learned that an unpleasant task doesn't get easier the longer you put it off. –AGE 35

• • •

I've learned that before you make fun of a certain car, make sure your boyfriend's parents don't own one. –AGE 19

• • •

I've learned that you're never too old to hold your father's hand. –AGE 11

I've learned that it's a good marriage when both mates think they got better than they deserve. –AGE 43

• • •

I've learned that I shouldn't keep dating my boyfriend just because he's good at fixing my car. –AGE 23

• • •

I've learned that when there's something unpleasant to do, do it first. –AGE 79

• • •

I've learned that all cars lose their new car smell no matter how much they cost. –AGE 29

I've learned that the "speedy service" signs at fast-food drive-through windows are there to make you laugh. —AGE 31

• • •

I've learned to appreciate home-cooked meals, especially the ones I don't have to cook. —AGE 38

• • •

I've learned that when your children complain about doing household chores, you simply tell them that they are either tenants or family members. If they're tenants, they pay rent; if they're family members, they assume responsibilities. —AGE 48

I've learned that when your children first get their driver's licenses, you are willing to drive them anywhere. —AGE 56

• • •

I've learned that you should never count your money while sitting in a moving car with the windows open. —AGE 27

• • •

I've learned that you don't have to keep running after you've caught the bus. —AGE 20

• • •

I've learned that to save yourself the price of a face-lift, smile a lot. —AGE 55

I've learned that I know there are angels around me protecting me, but sometimes I feel as if they're off duty. —AGE 12

• • •

I've learned that in old age you spend half your time looking for a bathroom and the other half trying to remember people's names. —AGE 65

• • •

I've learned that excellent service from someone deserves a letter written to that person's boss and a request that the letter be placed in the employee's personnel file. —AGE 31

I've learned that it's better to invite guests on a rainy day as dust doesn't show as much as when it is sunny. –AGE 65

• • •

I've learned that every day we are offered twice as many opportunities as problems.
–AGE 33

• • •

I've learned that you're never too old for a water gun fight. –AGE 19

• • •

I've learned that good habits are the shortest route to the top. –AGE 41

I've learned that the best answer my mother gave me as a child was "because I'm the mom, that's why." –AGE 25

• • •

I've learned that by the time I can afford it, I don't want it anymore. –AGE 56

• • •

I've learned that sometimes watching a child fail is the most painful but necessary thing a parent can endure. –AGE 48

• • •

I've learned that children stop being children, but you never stop being their mother. AGE 38

I've learned that simple truths remain and the things that really matter rarely ever change.

–AGE 56

. . .

I've learned that self-discipline, courage, and good character are impregnable to the assaults of bad luck. –AGE 47

. . .

I've learned that in a divorce, only the lawyers come out ahead. –AGE 37

. . .

I've learned that I do not have to be perfect all the time for my family to love me. –AGE 18

I've learned that I shouldn't waste my weekends by worrying about what faces me in the office on Monday. —AGE 28

• • •

I've learned that you should never let your four-year-old brother cut your hair. —AGE 11

• • •

I've learned that whoever said you can't buy happiness forgot about puppies. —AGE 28

• • •

I've learned that Thursdays are "yes" days. People are more open and relaxed and more favorable on Thursdays. —AGE 39

I've learned that grandmothers hate washing off those little fingerprints left by the precious little hands of their grandchildren. –AGE 65

• • •

I've learned that a best friend is someone who loves you when you forget to love yourself. –AGE 18

• • •

I've learned that the fastest way to get a green light is to start writing something down while you're at a red light. –AGE 42

• • •

I've learned that it's best to buy the expensive paint that covers in one coat. –AGE 29

I've learned that peeing in the woods with a couple of friends can be a real bonding experience. –AGE 20

• • •

I've learned as a life guard that when you throw nickels in the pool without anyone seeing you, it brings many smiles to the children who find them. –AGE 19

• • •

I've learned that I'd rather have a lot of brothers and sisters and not get many things than have no brothers and sisters and get everything. –AGE 13

I've learned that when you're looking for something, it's usually the last one in the pile.
–AGE 27

• • •

I've learned that the slowest lane of traffic is always the one I'm in.   –AGE 42

• • •

I've learned that sometimes the things that scare you the most turn out to be the best times of your life.   –AGE 20

• • •

I've learned that it's easy to be critical about something you've never experienced.   –AGE 51

I've learned that to really understand how much my father loves me, I needed to have a son. —AGE 30

• • •

I've learned that you should thank the salesclerks who take the time to compare the signature on your credit card with the signature on the receipt. —AGE 24

• • •

I've learned that going to the doctor's office is like going to church. You don't want to be late but you don't want to get there too early, either. —AGE 37

I've learned that everything I truly value has been gained by vulnerability on my part. It is the secret to life. —AGE 21

• • •

I've learned that just because you've gotten in the last word doesn't mean you've won the argument. —AGE 61

• • •

I've learned that my mom smells better when she doesn't have perfume on. —AGE 10

• • •

I've learned that trying to smile while saying "soy sauce" will always make you laugh. —AGE 20

I've learned that by the time you retire and draw social security, everything you have either hurts or doesn't work.   –AGE 66

• • •

I've learned that when the duties of being a teacher overwhelm me, my students almost always brighten my day in some small way.
–AGE 39

• • •

I've learned that you should never blow a big bubble with your gum if your head is out the window of a car going 40 mph and you have long hair.   –AGE 18

I've learned that when I'm alone in my room, I
have a beautiful singing voice. –AGE 16

The Complete Live and Learn and Pass It On

I've learned that no matter how busy someone is, they're never too busy to tell you how busy they are. −AGE 42

• • •

I've learned that it's just as important to be friendly to the janitor as it is to be friendly to the company president. −AGE 23

• • •

I've learned that work enjoyed is as much fun as leisure. −AGE 51

• • •

I've learned that I can't change the past, but I can let it go. −AGE 63

I've learned that no matter what time you decide to go to the bank, everyone else has decided to go then, too.   −AGE 28

• • •

I've learned that having extra time to spend with my children is more important than having extra money to spend on them.   −AGE 34

• • •

I've learned that kids will pretty much meet the expectations that you set for them.   −AGE 38

• • •

I've learned that when a woman says she's not mad, she usually is.   −AGE 24

I've learned that you never, ever wear an overpriced bridesmaid dress again at another event, no matter what the bride tells you.

–AGE 28

• • •

I've learned that when my dad says he's going to barbecue, it means we're going to have a burned piece of meat for supper. –AGE 13

• • •

I've learned that I'm glad I grew up in a poor household. It taught me that one doesn't need a lot of money to be happy and that there's an advantage to having to struggle a bit. –AGE 23

I've learned that when asking a child what he's up to, never believe the reply "Nothing."
–AGE 20

• • •

I've learned that arguing with a teenager is like mud wrestling a pig; you both get dirty and the pig loves it.   –AGE 48

• • •

I've learned that learning to laugh at yourself is the surest sign of maturity.   –AGE 47

• • •

I've learned that moms make mistakes too.
–AGE 16

I've learned that in twenty years no one is going to care about what I got on my biology final. –AGE 16

. . .

I've learned that no matter how many clothes I iron the night before, I will end up wearing something else. –AGE 28

. . .

I've learned that what people want most in life is to be loved and appreciated. –AGE 21

. . .

I've learned that life isn't fair; so accept it and adjust. –AGE 17

I've learned that sometimes you should just let your heart decide and deal with reality later.
–AGE 21

* * *

I've learned that God gives you a new gift every day. –AGE 7

* * *

I've learned that you should never leave a seven-year-old with a bat and ball alone by a window while baby-sitting him. –AGE 13

* * *

I've learned that sandwiches cut diagonally taste better. –AGE 38

I've learned that "yuck" is not the best response when your mom tells you what's for dinner. −AGE 12

• • •

I've learned that if you hang something in a closet for a while it shrinks two sizes. −AGE 62

• • •

I've learned that nothing tastes as good as being thin feels. −AGE 40

• • •

I've learned that whenever I get mad at my mom, I should try to remember that she loves me. −AGE 10

I've learned that peer pressure is just too much; when I'm alone, I'm a completely different person than I am at school. –AGE 12

• • •

I've learned that the way you speak of your spouse to others either builds up your family or casts a cloud over it. –AGE 58

• • •

I've learned that it's disastrous to forget your anniversary. –AGE 44

• • •

I've learned that one loss doesn't make a season. –AGE 52

I've learned that a great picker-upper is when I hear my grandchild say, "Come sit by me, Grandma." —AGE 60

• • •

I've learned that you should never give your brother the squirt gun when it's loaded with water. —AGE 7

• • •

I've learned that life is full of good surprises even if they do seem to come far apart. —AGE 58

• • •

I've learned that you can't give a hug without getting one in return. —AGE 36

I've learned that you should never take sides when your friends are upset with each other.
−AGE 13

• • •

I've learned that having someone tell you he loves you and having someone show you he loves you are two completely different things.
−AGE 18

• • •

I've learned that what makes me happiest is my son holding my face in his hands and telling me I'm the best mom he could ever have. −AGE 48

I've learned that it's a good idea to ask for the details before you say yes when someone asks, "Can you do me a small favor?" —AGE 37

• • •

I've learned that you always gain five pounds on the scale at the doctor's office. —AGE 12

• • •

I've learned that all your school pictures look good except the one in the yearbook that everyone sees forever. —AGE 14

• • •

I've learned that a dropped screw or nail in the garage becomes instantly invisible. —AGE 60

I've learned that
a good friend is better
than a therapist. —AGE 19

I've learned that you can't make friends by waiting for other people to step forward. You need to make the first move. —AGE 14

• • •

I've learned that my piano teacher gets a funny look on her face when she notices I haven't practiced. —AGE 11

• • •

I've learned that onion breath isn't bad when your spouse has it too. —AGE 32

• • •

I've learned that the copy machine can tell when I'm in a hurry. —AGE 20

I've learned that you should never teach your little brothers how to use a slingshot. –AGE 13

. . .

I've learned that you're never too old for slumber parties. –AGE 19

. . .

I've learned that there is a very crucial difference between charm and character.
–AGE 37

. . .

I've learned that grandparents can be just as much of a joy to their grandchildren as their grandchildren are to them. –AGE 18

I've learned that planning a vacation is sometimes just as much fun as experiencing it. –AGE 48

• • •

I've learned that my father lets me do things my mother would never even think about.
–AGE 13

• • •

I've learned that you shouldn't talk about what you're going to do. Do it, then talk. –AGE 49

• • •

I've learned that it's possible to fall madly in love with just one glance. –AGE 21

I've learned that there is no greater feeling of self-worth than when you help someone in need. —AGE 27

• • •

I've learned that receiving a thoughtful note or unexpected act of kindness from someone can make my day. —AGE 18

• • •

I've learned that the question parents hate the most is "Why?" —AGE 15

• • •

I've learned that chocolate is a food group.
—AGE 55

I've learned that while it's important to be my daughter's friend, it's more important to be her mother. —AGE 35

• • •

I've learned that I shouldn't change the channel when my dad's watching the Dallas Cowboys. —AGE 11

• • •

I've learned that sometimes a P.S. to a letter is the most important message of all. —AGE 14

• • •

I've learned that leisure isn't enjoyed unless it's been earned. —AGE 51

I've learned that it's the teacher and not the subject that makes a class interesting. –AGE 23

• • •

I've learned that parents always bring up those embarrassing childhood stories at all the wrong moments. –AGE 15

• • •

I've learned that competing with a friend over a man is a fun game unless one of you actually wins. –AGE 21

• • •

I've learned that I shouldn't call my identical twin sister ugly. –AGE 12

I've learned that having a boss who makes you sick isn't a terminal condition.   –AGE 47

• • •

I've learned that adolescence is a time of growing and experiencing. I just didn't know it would hurt so much.   –AGE 15

• • •

I've learned that nothing is better than coming home to a lit fireplace on a cold, snowy night and drinking hot chocolate.   –AGE 19

• • •

I've learned that because my parents believe in me, I believe in me.   –AGE 23

I've learned that when you go somewhere and they say "Don't bring valuables," DON'T BRING VALUABLES. –AGE 12

• • •

I've learned that you spend the first year of your children's lives trying to get them to walk and talk, then the rest of your life trying to get them to sit down and shut up. –AGE 41

• • •

I've learned that no matter how much work a husband does around the house, if he doesn't know how to give his wife affection, the marriage can go down the drain. –AGE 46

I've learned that imagining God standing beside me stops me from doing things I know are wrong. −AGE 15

. . .

I've learned that I get in trouble if I lick a lollipop, let my dog lick it, and lick it again.
−AGE 8

. . .

I've learned that when you take your girlfriend out for lunch and she orders the salad bar because she's on a diet, before the lunch is over, she'll eat half of your cheese fries. −AGE 46

I've learned that position can be bought, but respect must be earned. –AGE 51

• • •

I've learned that wherever I go, I should try to leave it either cleaner or happier than it was before I arrived. –AGE 19

• • •

I've learned that the best gift, to give or receive, is a book that touches the heart.

–AGE 25

• • •

I've learned that a little dog hair never hurt anybody. –AGE 79

I've learned that you should never fall in love at summer camp. It ends, but life goes on.

—AGE 17

• • •

I've learned that any cheap brownie mix can be good when chocolate chips are added to the batter. —AGE 34

• • •

I've learned that you have to kiss a lot of frogs before you find your prince. —AGE 28

• • •

I've learned that if you can laugh at yourself, you will always be amused. —AGE 31

I've learned that it scares me to walk in the bathroom and see my grandpa's teeth on the sink. —AGE 16

• • •

I've learned that money talks but all mine ever says is, "Good-bye." —AGE 13

• • •

I've learned that you should never put a rubber snake in your older brother's bed. —AGE 7

• • •

I've learned that your children can make you happier or madder than you've ever been in your life. —AGE 32

I've learned that you shouldn't write the name of whom you love really big on your new backpack that you have to wear to school every day. —AGE 12

• • •

I've learned that when a society accepts the premise that individuals are not responsible for their own actions, it's in real trouble.

—AGE 71

• • •

I've learned that it's hard to determine where to draw the line between being nice and not hurting people's feelings and standing up for what you believe. —AGE 12

I've learned that college isn't just about preparing for your future career, it is about finding out who you are right now. —AGE 23

• • •

I've learned that I love being a senior; it's graduation I'm worried about. —AGE 79

• • •

I've learned that no matter what mood I'm in, James Taylor is always perfect. —AGE 19

• • •

I've learned that life is like a book. Sometimes we must close a chapter and begin the next one. —AGE 34

I've learned that your best friend is the person who comes to your dance recitals and names goldfish after you. –AGE 14

. . .

I've learned that there are only two classes: first class and no class. –AGE 20

. . .

I've learned that giving doesn't count if you don't want what you're giving away. –AGE 11

. . .

I've learned that within each person is a treasure, but sometimes you have to dig for it. –AGE 32

I've learned that there are two places you are always welcome: church and Grandma's house. –AGE 12

• • •

I've learned that success is having money to pay the bills and still have enough to order a pizza without a coupon. –AGE 47

• • •

I've learned that no matter how much fun you have on vacation, the best part is coming home and sleeping in your own bed. –AGE 15

ACKNOWLEDGMENTS

My grateful thanks to all who contributed to this collection of discoveries and insights:

Volume One

Rosemary Brown, Adam Brown, Sallie Bett Crowell, Wade Watson, Shannon Stinson, Lori DeSanders, Emily Merriwether, Marian Meyerson, David Redford, Gifford Vance, Lee Wilson, Morris MacKenzie, Steven Curtiswood, Marnie Salyer, Franklin Powers, Oscar Liebman, Irene Copeland, Rusty Brakefield, Allan Rhodes, David and Jeanne Siefert, Marguerite Grady, Col. Henry Cullum, Warner Brooks, Patti Comini, Tony Gonzales, Houston Samuelson, Ann Wagner, Lenny Burkstrom, Helena Burnett, Rick and Mary Catherine Dobson, Jacob Selvin, Rupert Emerley, Paul Buchanan, Marc and Ann Talbot, Lisa Voss, Peter and Kathleen Lloyd, Tim and Stacy Donnally, Charles Cortez, Joanne Jacobson, Tab Quisenberry, Julie Cummings, Herman Agee, Matthew Conner, Paula Mitchell, Janet Burns, Michael

Combs, Paula Mitchell, Sol Shapiro, Rick Poland, Tom Roberts, Wes
Caplinger, Ben Caperton, Sissy Mills, Tucker Mayfield, Rev. Benson
Hopper, India Michaelson, C. M. Gatton, Esther Parker, Dr. Lambert
Lipscomb, Liz Murfree, Shelley Mellow, Rhoda Rettings, John Colbert,
Mildred Cooney, Gates Borman, Lennie Maxwell, Maj. Blakeley
Broadhurst, Carter Swain, Hazel Prince, Blanche DeSoto, Ed and
Pamela Stubblefield, Helen Naismith, Dennis Custer, Scott Turnbull,
Stephanie Lindsey, Fred O'Brien, Craig Biggart, Ed Hollas, Terrence
Bainbridge, Al Cunningham, Lassiter Bowling, Suzanne Bracey, Robert
Gross, Jarvis Jefferson, Lynn MacDermott, Randall Youngblood, Hilda
Grayson, Maynard Pembroke, Trisha Everly, Lisa Garvin, Don Spain,
Judith Rivers, Lori Murphy, Bill Beckman, Ted Armsley, Winnie
Cassady, Harold Boxwell, Philip Pershing, E. G. Falkner, Lester
Beauregard, O. C. Ramsey, Opal Ellis, Emily Donovan, Julie Jayne,
Jon Purnell, Arthur Singer, Al Peterson, Walt Weberman, Lee Wong,
Teenie Oakes, Wayne Stefan, Lester Short, Nate Henderson, Rod Guge,
Lorene Denton, Ben Jacobs, Charles Talbert, Flo Reeves, Sam Levine,
Mary Beth Simpson, Charlene Betts, Dale Diamond, Lillian Hartford,
Noel McCambridge, Carolyn Bally, Dot Oldfield, Oscar Mayhew, Myra
Sachs, Clyde Morrow, John Darwin, Jennifer Trumbull, Tom Glassman,

Larry Stone, Sue Head, Tricia Cummings, Bill Dreher, Eddie Tornquist, Vernon Redfield, Hank Holder, Estelle Farmer, Terry Hawkins, Vance Aldridge, Helene Ashley, Avery Barnes, C. C. Cash, DeWitt Berryman, Greg O'Toole, E. J. Volksman, Rod Milliken, Melinda Powers, Dede Marcus, E. M. Cheek, Tim Frickas, Phyllis Turner, Horace and Sarah Brown, Eloise Hensley, Louis Ripley, Shorty Thomas, Amy Bartley, Mary Beth McKinney, Sam Dennison, Daniel O'Donnell, Boris Beaman, Ruth Van Sykes, Chelly Fuson, Howard Stennis, Barbara Abernathy, Mabel Ruleman, Graham Waltham, Louise Redmon, Cecily Radnor, Linda LeFevre, Jay Sanders, Barry Oberlin, Brad Sprague, Max Draper, Dorothy Corbitt, Janette Hensley, Hunter Hastings, Pauline Espy, Ingrid Otterman, Caroline Raines, Randall Towers, Dwight Evans, Foster Francis, Brooke Schumacher, Tommy Cooper, Roger Bolding, Lee Ann Pasquo, Fern Williamson, Jackie Mayo, Albert Alvarez, Chip Thomas, Marietta Schofield, Jeffrey Tree, Tom Hodges, Rob Thomas, James Otto, Ginger Gill, Edward Champion, Sam and Lane Suppa, Kate Hamilton, Benjamin Good, Thomas Fielder, Joe Boone, Betsy Porter, Walter Graves, Ted Bannister, Mariah Newhouse, Fred Hutchinson, Aubrey Lassiter, Allan Ward, Dinah Pearlstone, Al Skinner, Lou Crutcher, Jeffrey Reynolds, Terry Goodin, Charles Milam, Evelyn Nunnelly,

Mario Minnelli, Beverlie Brewer, Ron Samuels, Kevin Ledbetter, M. S. Denby, Barry McAlister, Bob Seul, Steve Knotts, Shiela Volkert, Darlene Harrell, Herman Goodman, Melody Greene, Jan Blaustone, Diana McLaughlin, Stewart Fairfax, Heidi Wallace, Kevin Carney, Samuel Stern, Phil and Marge Kidd, Amy Field, Millie Hedgpeth, Burt Brandenberg, Colin Darwin, Elizabeth Griffin, Lance Deekner, Haley and Paige Rumore, Susannah McGavock, Sallye Schumacher, Cissy French, Ben and Lauren Saks, Bob Mullins, Roy Hightower, Bettye Jean Matthews, Roberta Whitman, Elizabeth Becker, Ed Collings, Mae Daly, Myra Helms, Glen Hollanger, Jack Sims, Helen Goodbody, Col. Williams MacLeod, Margaret Longino, Manley Briggs, Malcolm Ellington, Timothy Clark, Frank Cavenaugh, Joanne Copeland, Stan and Melisssa Crane, Vernon Quinlen, Rudy Kipp, Todd Batson, Olga Martindale, B. C. Lang, Tex Thompson, Gertrude Brown, Bill Satterwhite, Jim Ratcliff, Grace Weinstein, Red Cooley, Joyce Choate, Joe Lusky, W. D. McMurray, J. J. Rogers, Capt. R. V. Carleton, Judy Goins, David Goodman, Debbie Wallace Craig, Leigh Webster, Curtis Solo, Christopher Wray, C. A. Craig II, Tricia Holt, Dennis Taylor, Anne Overton, Casey O'Brien, Tim Schwendimann, Scott and Laurie Head, Effie Jones, Michael Spears, Carol Lockhart, Mary Bousman,

Eileen Mitchell, Paul Jay, Kim Chandler, Sol Heller, Bud Walters, Alexandria Main, Deidre Maddux, Katie, Blair, and Brien Rowan, Herb Kneeland, Addison Gore, Lisa Jones, Karen Freeman, Gertrude Brown, Doc Cline, Jill Martin, Martha DuBose, Owen Corello, Corrine Hall, Steven Yoo, Richard Speight, Richelle Melde, Merridith Ludwig, Nikole Mastroianni, Hollye Schumacher, Amy Zinman, Karl Weinmeister, Julie Levenberg, Paula Thompson, Kenneth Likely, Bonnie Smith, Doug Cooper, Beth Nicholson, Mitch Walters, John Burrows, Don Moore III, Ben Wilson, Anne Washburn, Shelby Applebaum, Sheri Tower, Bonnie Morales, and Edwin C. Hoover.

Volume Two

Rosemary Brown, Adam Brown, Anna Abraham, Angela Adair, Marilyn J. Adams, DeAnn Adelman, Sherri Allen, Steven Anderson, Joanne Anderson, June Anderson, Jeff Armes, Anna Marie Rose Atienza, Janice Anita Austin, Colleen Bailey, Peggy Baillie, Sean Baltz, John Bancheri, Dean Stanton Barnard Jr., Karin M. Basso, Laura Williams Bell, Amy Benedetto, Margaret Berardinelli, Nicholas Berlanga, Laura Bernell, Stacey Berry, David Betten, Jewell K. Bevan, Patricia Birmingham, Katie Blaschko, Frederika Blasko, Carol Bolno, Lois Boyd, Sandy

Bradbury, Betty Brady, Kristy Breedlove, Diana Britt, Beth Brochu,
Allison Brown, Betty Brown, Nancy Brown, Maryann Brummel,
Elizabeth Brunelle, Leslie Brydon, Karen Buchan, Yolanda Bucio,
Alice Buret, Chip Burns, Christopher Bursian, Marie Burt, Katy Butler,
Susan L. Butler, Lois Byrd, Laura Beth Byrnes, Peggy Byrnes, SuAnne
Cacamese, George E. Calfo, Jennifer Capone, Donna Canfield, Tree
Carel, Bea Carmody, Kate Carroll, Melissa Carroll, Joseph Carubia,
Douglas Casa, Mick Cassidy, Vincent Cautero, Jason Allen Cerezo,
Sharon Circ, Will Chappell, Patricia Citu, Laurie Kristin Clark, Rebecca
Cohen, Kasey Cole, Noni Coleman, Marilynn Collins, Jean Coneff,
Ransom Converse, Karl L. G. Crose, Kelly L. Crowford, Erin Cox,
Susanne Cox, Elektra Athena Dalrymple, Debbie Davidson, Kellie
Dawson, Peggy Lee Dean, Jerry Deatherage, Stacia Deedrick, Michelle
C. Defatta, Kristin June DeGiso, Virginia DeMars, Lawrence Dikeman,
David W. Donovan, Deborah Dougherty, Deborah L. Dougal, Gwyndolin
DuBose, Patricia Dugert, Cynthia Eichengreen, Vivian Elbert, Mary
A. Elliot, Elanor Emerson, Kathy Emswiler, Lucille Everingham,
Catie Fain, Donny Ferritto, Rebecca Fillmore, Dawn Finley, Mary E.
Finnerty, Vi Fishbaugh, Lisa Fischer, Ila Foley, Dana Ford, Robert Fox,

Florence Freedman, Carolyn Jane Freeman, Edna B. Frisbie, Robert P. Fullmer, Karen Funkhouser, Jane Ellen Gaines, Jeannie George, Lisa Giaramita, Suanna Gibson, Mrs. Clayton Gillette, Selina Gilliam, Arlene Glass, Kristina Glicksman, Adam Goertzen, Judith Goodchild, Barbara Goodman, Cathy Gorsuch, Diane Grabhorn, Mary Grabowski, Mary Row Gravely, MaryBeth Greaney, Cynthia Green, Mary Jo Grill, Jo Marie Grinkiewicz, Eileen Gromada, Ricky Groom, Karl Grose, Teresa Gunter, Ruth Hahner, Robert Haley, Shannon Halley, Joyce Hanes, Carla Hanks, Ndala G. Harper, Walt Harper, Albert Harris, Holly Haukaas, Mary Haynes, Margaret Hedlund, Lynn Hellman, Robert Hendrick, H. A. Henrich, Chip Herin, Daisy Hersey-Orr, Sage Holben, Julie Horkheimer, Bernilda Hoth, Frederick Hovey Jr., Nicole Howard, Diana Hughes, Martin Hughes, Kellie Huse, Janet Jackson, Tammy Jackson, Susan Jeffery, Francis Johnson, Gala Jones, Holly Jones, Jennifer Jones, Shirley Jordan, Anitura Joseph, Regina Joy, Stacy Judd, Robert Jutte-Kraus, Jenne Keller, Ruth S. Kelley, Paige Kepner, Dawn King, Karie Kinskey, Paul Koehler, Meredith Lynn Kohut, Erin Kossoris, Kenneth Kovac, Alisa Krintz, Tracy L. Kundinger, Edna B. Laine, Jessie Lang, Robert LaPlante, Amy Lazarus, Angela Lechtel, Shanna Lewis,

Lucy Limberis, Judity A. Lindberg, Brandon Long, Elizabeth Lopato, Linda Lopes, Estela Lugo, Patricia Lukoschek, Greg Lumpkin, Nicole Lusby, Wendy Lutz, Tiana Lyles, Heather Lytwyn, Ryan MacMichael, Colleen Magistad, Jason Malay, Susan Masaitis, Diana K. Mason, M. C. Martindale, Mari-Job Maulit, Kathy Maurer, Susan May, Greg Mayer, Susan Mayer, Sarah McBride, Shirley McCallum, Betty McClure, Kellian McDermott, Teresa McDowell, Gyneth McGarvey, Pam McGee, Cynthia N. McGivern, Pat McGovern, Kellie McInnis, Maureen McKenzie, Alline K. McNeil, Joan McQuerry, Susan Mechler, Maureen Melia, Imy Menser, Sylvia Moffett, Frances Miller-Papenfuss, Lara L. Milne, Sunshine D. Montgomery, Lynn Moore, Michelle Morgan, Kristi Morse, John Mortes, Julia Mulane, Hillary Munn, Sarah Ann Nelson, Michael Kelly Newsome, Anh Nguyen, Kim Nicely, Darcy Nichols, Irene Noraas, Meg Northcut, Jack Nussbaum, Kimberly Olson, Joan Onzo, Raymond J. Ormand, Irene Packard, Esther B. Palmer, Lucille Parker, Madeline Parker, Lena Parmiter, Florence Paulie-Healy, Amy Peacher, William Peredina, Jo Carole Peters, Adam Phillips, Wendy Pitlik, Nikki Plant, John Preston, Dan Prezembel, Lisa Quatrini, Carrie Rahm, Elizabeth Rakowski, Karen Reinerston, Janelle Rice, Stephanie

Robson, Pat Rodgers, Peter Rogers, Jolynn Ruud, Janice H. Ryan, Rene Rylander, Frances Sagona, Theresa Salak-Fawcett, Christine Sales, Fred Salter, Judy Sawyer, Vassa Scales, Eva Schmitz, Darch Schouw, Burton Schwartz, Rick Schwab, Drew Searing, Kelly Seelye, Elise Selinger, Eleanor Wright Shabica, Nell Shaffer, Carol Shahla, Eric S. Sherman, Ruby E. Shine, Shannon M. Skroback, Jean Slight, Cynthia Snell, Laurie Lynn Snyder, Paula Snyder, Andrew Sopko, Diane Spangler, Jane Spens, Cindy Standlee, Liz Starke, Amy Diane Steiner, Audrey L. Steiner, Jacquelyn Stone, Bob Sullivan, Valerie Susser, Katy Swann, Jennifer Swanson, Tara Swanson, Erika Sweek, Keri Sweet, Kelly Tankersley, Beth Theriot, Stephanie Tignor, Rick Tobe, Beverly Tomsic, Christine E. Torres, Frances S. Townes, Tami Tronick, Naohiko Tsukada, Kendia Turnbow, Terry Tyson, Nancy Vanhamel, Ricky Villabona, Pat Wade, Mark Walker, Kristine Wallace, Janet M. Wasilewski, J. Avis Waaterbury, Erika L. Watt, Shirley Watts, Carol Webster, Rachel Wehner, Eric Welch, Tami Westhoff, Jerry White, Carol Lynn Whiteley, Elissa Wickman, Rebecca Wiley, Paula Williams, Eleanor Wilson, Erica Wilson, Jennifer Winters, Darryl Wisher, Abby Wood, Kelly Workman, Heather Wrigley, Jennifer C. Wroe, and Lynn Younglove.

Volume Three

Anna Abraham, Janie Adams, DeAnn Adelman, Silvia Alba, Mary Allen, Diane Amadruto, Katarina Arguinzoni, Jeff Arney, Janice Austin, Bree Barton, Eileen Bassirl, Corinne Belsky, Jessica Berg, Rolanda Bertz, Jessica Bette, Laura Bogdas, Annie Borger, Linda Boyd, Joanne Bozue, Bill Brabbin, Alda Bradkoski, Carol Brandes, Antonio Bravo, Florence Brewis, Jasper Brewster, Dolores Brough, Amy Brown, Betty Brown, Jennifer Bruce, Mary Brunson, Marissa Bucci, Kay Burger, Therese Burke, Pat Bush, Elsa Campbell, Tom Candalino, Gerry Cantrell, Bea Carmody, Mel Cason, Megan Cassidy, Louise Cherry, Courtney Christopher, Sherry Cleaves, Shirley Clyburn, Michael Comprola, Joseph Connelly, Marie Cook, Suzanne Cook-Riddle, Christi Cotham, John Crawford, Brenda Crawley, Michelle Creason, Ann Crews, Timothy Cuff, Cali Cunningham, Alex Curio, Mary Cuthbert, Kathy Dalton, Nicole Darling, Angela Davies, Anne Davis, Delbert Davis, Sally Davis, David Debter, Lawrence Dikeman, Cathleen Donovan, Jennifer Draksler, Norma Duckett, Ruby Edwards, Don Eisenberg, Mary Elliott, Lorraine Failla, Melissa Ferrarese, Amie Fiedler, Virginia FitzSimmons, Sylvia Flowers, Darcy Fournier, Robert Fox, Rob Foxworthy, Carolyn Freeman,

Corissa Frericks, Janelle Froelich, Christine Gardner, Ildiko Gaspar, William Gates, Jeannie George, Sam Goldsmith, Michelle Gomez, Dawn Goodrich, Mary Grabowski, Kara Green, Dennis Guadalupe, Renee Haines, Sylvia Hamilton, Alice Haney, Catherine Hardy, Walt Harper, Dennis Harrington, Jeffrey Harrington, Rita Harris, Holly Haukaas, Lois Hausner, Lisa Hay, Dorothy Hella, Krystal Henagan, Brenda Henry, Heidi Hildebrand, Chrystal Hinz, Bill Hockaday, Jane Holding, Berdyne Hoover, Kathleen Howell, Jacqueline Hudnell, Nikia Huffman, Jake Hughes, Scott Hummer, Holly Hutchins, Jennifer Johnson, Laurie Johnson, Lindsey Johnson, Lori Johnson, Ann Jolliffe, Wesley Jones, Courtney Judd, Michael Julien, Karen Karp, Lindsay Katal, A. Katin, Jenne Keller, Sandy Kenslow, Mark Kern, Shawn Kerstetter, Fatimah Khan, Kathryn Kiebler, Chelsey Knauer, Judith Kopec, Paul Kostansek, Susan Kratzenberg, Kristen Krugeinhard, Tracy Kundinger, Brenda Laird, Eden Langewis, Christopher Lawless, Evelina Lawrence, Angela Lechter, Rachel Lee, Alison Lipari, Lori Lipton, Robert Lott, Patricia Lukoschek, Wanda Lynn, Lynn Madden, Suzanne Mailloux, Jana Marine, Glenn Martin, Marion Martin, Meaghan Martin, Angela Maschari, Terry Masek, Shelley Mason, Kevin Masser, Katherine

Massey, Marco Matute, Susan Mayer, Leah Mazar, Joseph McCue, Patrick McGlashan, Brant McKeever, Chalonne McLeod, Rebecca McMichael, Alline McNeil, Franklyn McWay, Sherry Meadows, Megan Meeker, Imy Menser, Kimberley Mentes, Alexis Michael, M.A. Moldenhauer, Sherwood Moran, Maureen Mosley, Julia Mullane, Phyllis Muller, Hilary Munn, Jennifer Murfin, Jill Murphy, Michelle Murphy, Kathy Nadason, Becky Newcomb, Ema Newcomb, Titi Nguyen, Kristina O'Brien, Misty O'Dell, Tess Oakes, Shelby Oberstein, Deborah Obrecht, Robin Osborne, Jamie Osman, Susan Osso, Kelley Paige, Ann Pate, Kimberly Peek, Candy Penner, Michelle Pennock, Wendy Pierret, Grace Piper, Kris Placencia, Claire Pocock, Sharon Popovich, Tom Porter, Laura Poulson, Chris Proffitt, Kaye Prouty, Vanessa Ray, Cynthia Read, Brian Rees, Jenny Rehbein, Cindy Reisinger, Liz Rice, Erika Rickard, Jennifer Ristic, Lynn Robards, Brian Robinson, Celeste Rodriguez, Brenda Roe, Chris Rogers, Patti Rosenswie, Tamara Ross, Carrie Rossetti, Spencer Royer Jr., Sheri Sarsfield, Steve Saunders, James (Sam) Sawyer, June Sawyer, Lacie Saxton, Amy Schaffer, Nora Schill, Carrol Schroyer, Janie Schuelka, Justin Seibel, Elise Selinger, Kevin Shaffer, Carla Shasteen, Ruby Shine, Stephanie Sicoia, Steve Siglar, Shannon

Skroback, Dana Slocomb, Kerry Smith, Lindsay Smith, Terri Smith, Susan Soderquist, Kat Sproule, Lucille St. Pierre, Cecilia Stamas, Edwin Steinsapir, Jaime Stoddard, Elizabeth Stone, Leta Stratton, Brenda Streatch, Susan Stulen, Maria Stutzman, Teresa Summerville, Michelle Sumovich, Kara Svendsen, Angela Swann, Kelly Taney, Stephani Tennant, Ashley Thomas, David Thomas, Kris Thommesen, Janice Thompson, Betty Trimm, Ann Troy, Heather Tygrett, Joyce Van Deusen, Hollie Van Kirk, Karla Venis, Catherine Vodrey, Stephanie Vosmus, Lisa Vrana, Elizabeth Vukovitch, David Wacker, Janet Wasilewski, Libby Waterbury, Shirley Watts, Lori West, Carol Whiteley, Bobbie Whitlock, Eric Wicktor, Stefanie Wielkopolan, Cynthia Williams, Eva Williams, Claudia Wineke, Kari Winter, Availr Woodward, Wayne Wyler, Janet Yeakley, Danielle Zarda, Hilary Zetlen, Molly Ziebell, and Catalina Zobel.

Dear Reader,

If life has taught you a thing or two and you would like to pass it on, please write to me. I would welcome the opportunity of sharing it with other readers.

Thank you.

H. Jackson Brown, Jr.
P.O. Box 150014
Nashville, TN 37215

www.instructionbook@aol.com